Two Saints & a Lot of Us Sinners
The History of one of Ireland's Oldest Inhabited Castles

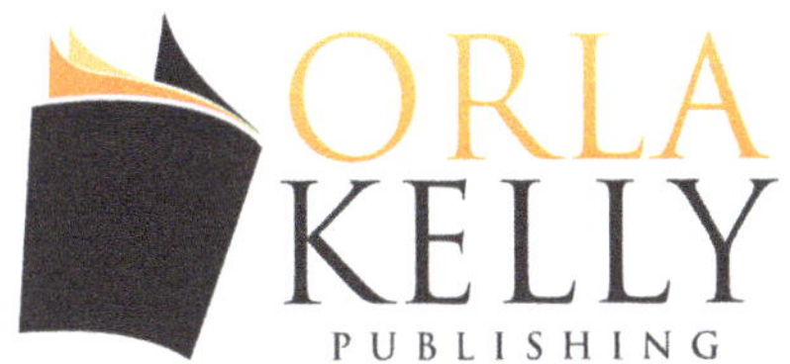

Brian Donovan Thompson

First published in the Republic of Ireland in 2020.

 This book is based on the author's historical document interpretation and memoirs from the author on Cloghan Castle when it was under owndership of the author. The authors views are his own. Photographs used from the authors personal archive and from other sources who kindly provided images for the book. These are credited in the publication as are other historical reference sources quoted from. This castle is now under private ownership and is not open to the public.

ISBN 978-1-912328-59-8 (paperback edition)

Published by Orla Kelly Publishers, Cork, Ireland. Edited by Catherine Robinson.

Orla Kelly Publishing
27 Kilbrody, Mount Oval
Rochestown, Cork
Ireland

Elyse

My beloved wife, who out of necessity transformed a castle into our home.

Without your encouragement, these jottings would never have seen the light of day

Contents

Index of Images

Foreword

I knew Brian Thompson a year or two before I actually met him. I don't mean that I knew *of* him … I knew the man … the essential man, himself. And it came about like this:

In the mid-seventies of the last century we bought a house in Banagher that needed a lot of repair and maintenance. I asked the town's main supplier of building material, Frank Brennan, for the name of a craftsman who might help us. Frank gave me a name, adding, "If you want to talk to him, he's working in Lusmagh, at Cloghan Castle." I drove out there at once.

Even from half a mile away, pausing on the drive to take in the setting and get the measure of the actual building, I realised I was seeing something rare and splendid in the long history of Irish domestic-military architecture: The owner was restoring *the outer walls*! Four centuries ago a follower of Oliver Cromwell had *slighted* those bastions to ensure that the castle would never again serve any military purpose. And every owner since had meekly accepted the slight.

But not this man – this new owner. I did not know his name then, but I knew the cut of his jib. To him a castle was a mere eunuch of a building without its proper defences; but no castle with his name on the title should live with them reduced to mere ragged foundations. In fact, as the quare fella on site told me, this Brian Thompson had even improved the principal wall with the addition of a sentry walk and new gatehouse of his own design.

It was an act of love and reverence, of course – the sort of love and care he has given to so many properties throughout his life … and it doesn't stop there, for he has now carried it onward into this magnificently loving history of the demense he did so much to rescue, enhance, and leave to the glory of this land and nation.

Malcolm Ross-Macdonald

Author of the Stevenson saga books

Preface

When one comes to write a history book, no matter how small, one is faced with a problem which is difficult to overcome. We tend to write in the language of today with the prejudices of today. The result is that the rebels of the past have become the heroes of the present and history is often viewed through the eyes and viewpoints of the author.

I have, therefore, tried to see that as much as possible in this book, the writings are of different times and express the attitudes held in the past.

History is, of course, now history and when written down for posterity, its narrative should not be one-sided, although it almost invariably is.

What happened to this particular castle over the centuries gives us an idea of what happened to the whole country.

Ireland has changed quite incredibly in the past twenty years, and we have never been better fed, better educated, better housed, and better clothed.

If, without bitterness, we can go from our centrally heated homes to an excellent local supermarket to enjoy the good things of today without forgetting our heritage, then – we as a nation are growing up.

When I think of the men, women and children who starved to death in the locality within the memory of my Great Grandmother, then I would like to think that they would be proud of what we have achieved.

Brian Donovan Thompson
Cloghan Castle
Lusmagh
Banagher
County Offaly
Ireland
2001

Acknowledgments

I should like to thank the following, without whose help this book would never have been finished, let alone written:

To my beloved daughter Rosalind Fanning, whose enthusiastic discovery of a newspaper advertisement for the sale of this castle, while still a school boarder in Dublin, directly influenced my purchase in 1972, and to my talented son Henry Thompson for his knowledgeable assistance in the physical restoration work of Cloghan. Thank you for your continued support.

To my stepdaughters whom I love as my own: Daphine Aikens and her husband Tim for their help and their generosity in financially rescuing the castle; Stephanie Newton and her husband Nigel for their helpful support over the years; Catherine Robinson and her husband Henry for their thoughtful help, and for transforming my handwritten scribbles into this printed book.

Mrs Vicki (Moore) Jacobs, Egerton Skipwith, Max Rowland, Mrs Tita Madden (wife of Dr James Madden, probably The O'Madden), Margaret and Norman Anderson, Denis Kelly, Stan and Jan Shelton, Mrs N G Aitken, Professor K W Nicholls, Mrs Margaret Barton, Mrs Margaret Graves, Marjorie and Dermot Graves, Dr John Fleetwood, Helen Burton, Mr John Coakley – Lecturer, University College Dublin, Tina Claffey Photography, the award-winning nature photographer, for kindly taking these sale brochure pictures and later helping us to use them here, and Richard Surman Photograhy, for generously permitting us to share from his book *Castle Cats of Britain & Ireland.*

And to the memories of the late Valerie Landon; the late Mr Paddy Kelly; the late Mrs Pamela Whiteford; and the late Lt Col Denis James Daly.

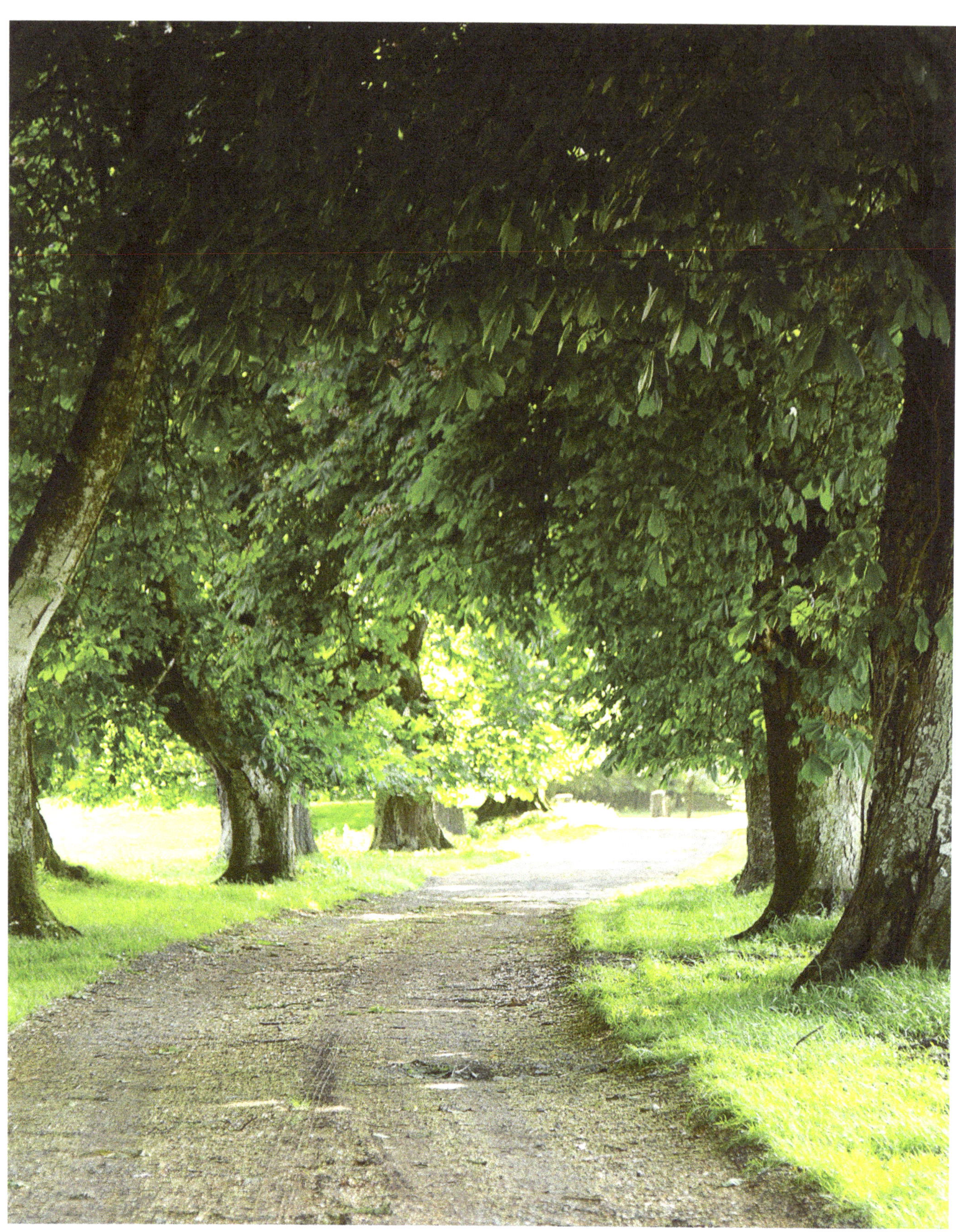

Mile Long Driveway with Chestnut Trees

Introduction

This is the story of Cloghan Castle, Lusmagh, in County Offaly. It is believed to be one of the oldest continuously inhabited Irish castles in the country, and it rests on an ancient monastic site dating back 1,400 years.

The book covers the entire period of its existence from once being a vast estate to a quaint old house set in lovely parkland in a mere 157 acres. It also describes how the Irish author, a founding member of the Historic Houses Association of England, bought it in 1972 from Major and Mrs Bowes-Daly, restored its crumbling foundations, and lived in it with his second wife and stepfamily until its sale to international owners in 2018.

The book starts with a Bronze Age dagger found in the front park, the monastery of St Cronin and its pilgrimage walk to Clonmacnoise, the arrival of the Normans, and the capture of the land in battle in 1336 by the famous Prince and Clan Chief, Eoghan of the O'Maddens.

There are intriguing documented stories about the 1595 siege by Elizabethan forces, social and political links with the nearby, and influential, Birr Castle, and nationally historic events through the lives of the various owners.

In the seventh century, St Cronan founded a monastery at Cloghan and for over a millennium this site commanded a strategic position on one of the main trade routes across the River Shannon - a gateway between the western and eastern provinces.

The Normans held the property between 1203 and 1336 when it was taken by the Gaelic Chief Eoghan O'Madden. The castle as we see it today was built by the O'Madden Clan who eventually conceded to English rule under the Elizabethan armies in 1595. The castle figured in the Elizabethan (1595) Cromwellian (1650) and Jacobite (1689) wars. Parts of the castle were remodelled down through the years and the cathedral hall was added in the latter half of the eighteenth century.

Prior to 1972, there had been on the land two Irish Saints, a Norman Sinner (William de Burgo) Irish Chieftains and a Norman family of Moores who became very Irish and were awarded three Victoria Crosses, Dr Graves who discovered thyroid disease, and other notables.

In summary, this book is a mix of legend and potted history about an enchanting Desmesne with yew trees dating back 1,000 years, its solidly built Irish castle and its place in history.

Chapter 1

Pre-History

Pre-History

In ancient times, Ireland was a land of forests, lakes, rivers, bogs and swamps. It was not easy to move around except by boat and on a few well-defined roadways. Esker stone ridges made ideal roadways and Shallows made excellent crossing points for large rivers.

The felling of trees must have been an enormous task thousands of years ago and we can well understand why Lusmagh was a suitable area for settlement.

The winter-flooded Callows gave ample grazing in the Summer and in Winter there would have been up to 100,000 wild birds, Lapwing, Duck, Geese and Swans, which could have been trapped with the use of nets and decoys to provide winter food.

An early Bronze Age dagger beside a human skeleton has been found in the Cloghan castle demesne leading one to believe that the site has been occupied for 5,000 years.

From the 7th century onwards, Monks would have tilled the substantial area around what is now Cloghan Castle. By the 12th century, the farms would have been a considerable size. Remnants of these ancient habitations abound.

The Esker Ridge provided the roadway from the east to the shallow Shannon River Crossing at Meelick. This was the possible site for a monastery or a castle. To this day, the "old road" is an atmospheric part of the demesne.

CLOGHAN CASTLE

The word 'Cloghan' in Irish means the following:

A row of stepping stones

A stony ford

An old stone structure

A stone house, cell or small stone church

Stony land

A cluster of small stone buildings

Ancient Irish monasteries were usually a cluster of small stone houses. Five hundred years ago Cloghan Castle was known as O'Madden's Stone castle.

LUSMAGH

Lusmagh means 'The Plain of Healing Herbs'.

HY MANY

The ancient territory ruled by the Kellys, their kinsmen the O'Maddens and, at one stage, the MacCoughlans.

A MOST 'CASTLED' COUNTRY

One of the most striking man-made features of the Irish countryside is the amount of castles. They range in size from tiny tower houses to huge stone structures. There were very few castles built in Ireland prior to the Normans, who built them to subdue the population. The Irish, however, thought castles a great idea and developed their own smaller versions. It was originally thought that there were 2,000 of them built, but further research has greatly increased this estimate to 3,500 and more.

At least 500 of these could be restored and lived in.

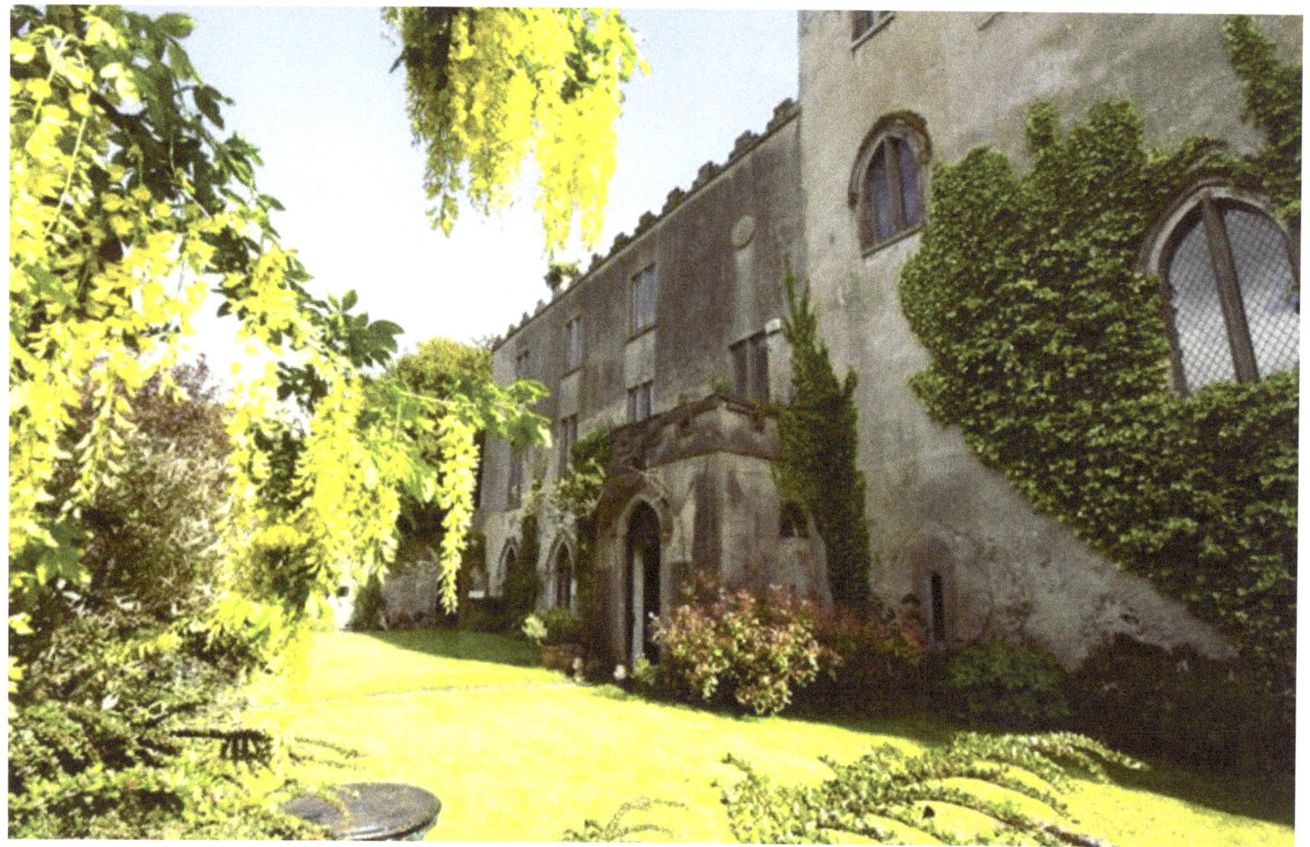

Front Courtyard

Chapter 2

Early History of Cloghan Castle 600-1204

Early History Of Cloghan Castle

600 - 1204

Legend has it that Saint Cronan established a monastery in Lusmagh 1,400 years ago and that Cloghan Castle now sits on that site. It is even thought that the original stone cell of the saint was incorporated within the existing keep as a sentry post.

We know that in ancient times there were only four main crossings of the Shannon River apart from the bridge at Clonmacnoise. They were Limerick, Killaloe, Meelick and Athlone. The main highway went from Dublin to Roscrea, branched off to Birr and went over the Esker Ridge to Lusmagh. The ridge ceases at Cloghan Castle and the road went on to the Shannon shallows at Meelick. It does not take a great deal of imagination to work out that the old Esker road was a link between the monasteries.

The Normans came into the area in 1203. It is known that William De Burgo built a defensive mote and Bailey round the church at Meelick and advanced into Lusmagh. It is highly probable that he built a defensive wall around the remains of St Cronan's monastery, and the existing wall around the old Yew garden would appear to have been built at the same time. In my opinion, this was the beginning of the life of Cloghan Castle.

We know that the Normans were here for over 100 years and were finally expelled by the O'Maddens in 1336. History tells us that Eoghan O'Madden defeated the 'Men of Ormonde' in two great battles in Lusmagh. Eoghan was married to a De Burgo Norman and the 'Men of Ormonde' were the Norman De Butlers, who controlled the territory to the south of Lusmagh.

1336 was the year that Mac Egan built Redwood castle (three miles from Cloghan Castle) and Eoghan O'Madden was a noted builder of castles. His family remained in possession of the castle that he almost certainly built, until 1595.

The Moore family who took over Cloghan castle in 1601 did not finally leave until 1852. They claimed that the castle was Norman, as did their successors who also claimed that the castle was on the site of St Cronan's monastery.

In my opinion, the O'Maddens built the present keep sometime after 1336. The castle is Irish, not Norman.

Saint Cronan & The Legend of The Book of Dimma

The Book of Dimma, which is called a 'pocket Gospel' is over 1,000 years old and has been carefully preserved for hundreds of years in the Library of Trinity College, Dublin. Historians have established that this precious manuscript was most likely created by a local monk. However…

Although the Book of Dimma was created in one of the monasteries previously founded by St Cronan, it was in Roscrea, just over a five-hour walk away from Lusmagh, and it was written in the 8th century, rather than as an earlier contemporary of St Cronan and not even written by Dimma after all!

Unfortunately, for some decades, unbeknown to us, we were enjoying the local legend that the Book of Dimma may have been written *here* on this very Demesne, in the 7th century, at the behest of St Cronan himself. After all, the original site of this particular Cloghan Castle was once one of St Cronan's monasteries, situated on the pilgrimage walk towards Clonmacnoise.

Here follows an extract from Reverend John Gleeson's book *History of Ely O'Carrol* first published in 1915, which lent credence to our local legend. He was, in turn, using the *Latin Life of St Cronan* from *Vitae Sanctorum Hiberniae*, edited by the respected historian Charles Plummer in 1910. Gleeson writes,

> *"St Cronan did not long remain in the province of Connaught. He crossed the Shannon (with a natural desire to return to his own country) and made a considerable stay in Lusmagh – probably the place where he wrote the famous book of Dimma. On one occasion, being in a wood the servant of God saw a deer passing by. He called the deer to him and when it came tamely, it ate an apple from his hand and departed quietly on its way at the order and by the permission of the saint."*
>
> The Latin Life of St Cronan continues, *"in the place before mentioned, Lusmagh, … There was a countless multitude of demons, who filled the entire place, as if it was their own house, in such a way that no person could live there before St Cronan. The holy father, Cronan, bravely entered into war with them in the name of the omnipotent God; and by the grace of Christ, he expelled them from that place to the end of the world. And from that day, they neither do harm nor appear there."*

Before leaving Lusmagh, the saint founded several missions. His influence with local chieftains was great, and this enabled him to secure sites for churches and oratories. He passed his Lusmagh Monastery on to his cousin (also a saint) called Mochanna. There is an illuminating story told of Cronan. Upon his departure from Lusmagh with all his followers – he made the decision to send one of them back to remain *"because he had not left all his belongings behind, but had brought a spade."*

> Reverend Gleeson continues *"It is stated that the Book of Dimma was written at the command of St Cronan in the monastery which he established in the Parish of Lusmagh. During the centuries*

that preceded the discovery of printing, the monks multiplied copies of the bible. The Book of Dimma is a copy of the Four Gospels.

A legend has come down to us regarding the writing of this book. St Cronan sought the services of a skilled scribe. Dimma was a skilled writer, but when asked by Cronan to do this work, he replied that the task would require much time and that he had but a single day to spare. Cronan told him to write on until the sun had set. Dimma wrote during forty days and nights without ceasing, without food, drink or sleep. He finished the writing of the Four Gospels, believing that he had written but for a single day. Such is the legend.

During the editing of this book, an internet search of Trinity College, Dublin, brought up the following note by a Research Fellow as to how and why the pocket Gospel would have been attributed to Dimma:

"The reason for the alteration would have been to enhance the holy nature of the book by connecting it to an episode from the life of Saint Cronan (d. 619), the founder of the Roscrea monastery...... Whoever wrote the name of Dimma over that of the original scribe, wished to transform this manuscript into the famous Gospels; the alteration was probably made at Roscrea in the late 10th or 11th century. Luckily, one colophon was left intact, on p. 103, revealing the original name of Dianchride, a name that occurs in the genealogy of the Ui Chorcrain, who had a branch based in the northern part of Tipperary." (Yvard, C. TCD, 2015)

Well, now we know. It is a bit deflating that Dimma's book was not written here. On the other hand, there is many a liminal moment when, during a simple stroll in the Cloghan Castle Demesne, even in the 21st century, the events of St Cronan's life appear... not *quite* so fantastical.

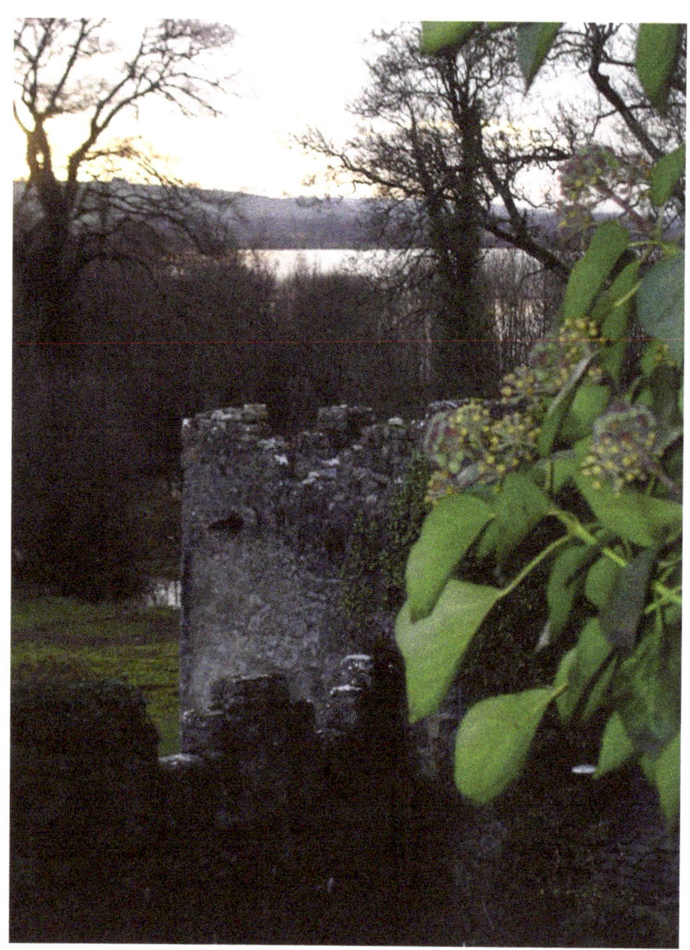

View of the back wing from the first floor

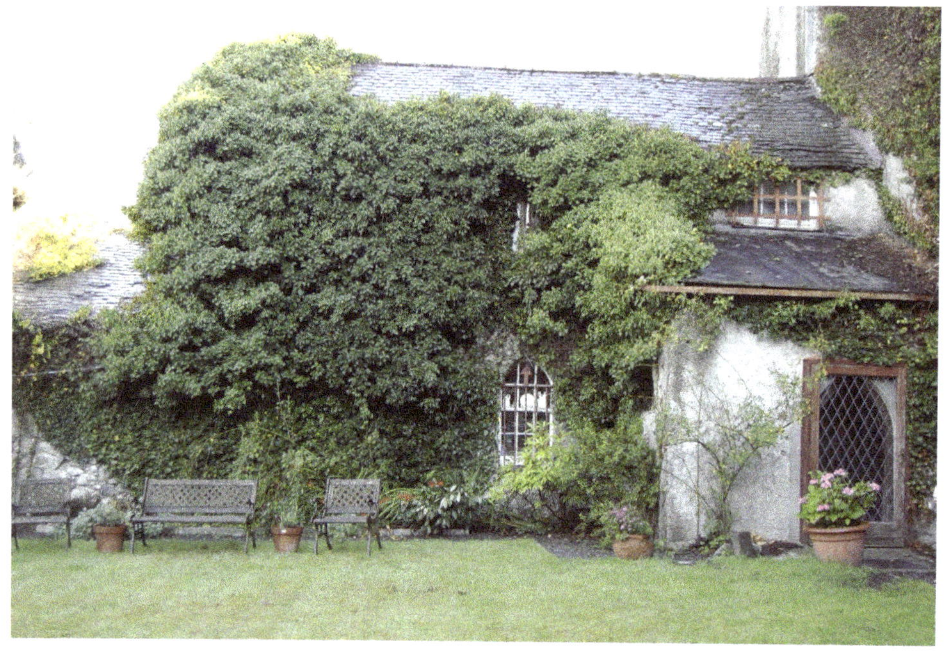

View of the oldest wing from one of the walled gardens

Chapter 3

Raths

Raths

There are the remains of three raths beside the front drive to Cloghan Castle. A Stone Age fortification and rath is clearly visible to this day at the top of a hill, south of the castle, on the other side of the Little Brosna River. The following is another extract from Reverend Gleeson's book, 'History of Ely O'Carroll'.

'The Irish Lords and Kings of the Milesian period built a few stone castles before the coming of the Anglo-Normans. At Tara, there was a resident population of five thousand persons; this number being immensely increased on the occasion of the great gatherings which will be described later on; and on the occasion of warlike hostings, which were frequent in those days.

The abundance of wood in the oak forests of Ireland was the reason why that material was so frequently used in the erection of dwellings, the most common kinds being deal and oak.

It should be understood that buildings of dry stone without mortar existed from the most remote times, such as the great fort of Dun Aengus in Aranmore. The wooden homes of the Irish were usually circular, but in some cases, they were oblong, like the banqueting hall of Cormac Mac Art, at Tara, which accommodated one thousand guests, erected in the third century before the coming of St Patrick.

The construction of the rath was simple. Around the inner circular mound, stout poles were fixed in the ground, standing near each other. Those poles were called ***slat.*** *The poles were peeled and polished smooth and were interwoven with hazel boughs. The surface of the wall was plastered and made brilliantly white, though it was sometimes striped in colours. The white poles were exposed to view. The poles were drawn together at the top in a beehive construction, leaving an opening at the top for the egress of smoke.*

The use of the wood as fuel in those days lessened the inconvenience of the smoke, while the centre part of the floor of the rath seems to have been raised some feet above the ordinary level, with a hollow place on top to receive the fire. Round this fire in the centre, reclining on straw or couches, the family lived in the smaller raths. In the larger raths, there were several apartments. The smaller rods used in the construction of a rath were called ***caelach*** *(slender); the hurdles or laths were called* ***chath*** *(cleea). Ara Claith means Ara of the wattled raths.*

In the better class of raths, the furniture, made of yew, was often ornamented with gold, bronze and gems. This fact is gathered from the Brehon Law and from the ancient records. The sloping roof of the rath, when large, was supported by a ***tuireadh,*** *or strong pole resting on the centre of the floor. This roof was composed of various materials, straw, thin boards and lead. The roof covering of ladies'* *greenans, or summerhouses, was sometimes covered with the wings of birds of different colours. The principal room was lighted by lamps, which were strung from a pole. The raths were supplied with windows and skylights having glass. The knocker was a hard piece of wood, called bas-chrann. Visitors always knocked with the bas-chrann.*

Locks were used in early times, as mentioned in the life of St Columba in the fifth century. Mention is also made of ***aradh,*** *or ladder. An outer circular mound called the lis surrounded the inner circle, on which the rath was raised. This rampart was planted on top with a close hedge for shelter and protection against wild animals and enemies.*

Outside the door of the rath, there was an ornamental green, called ***aurla,*** *sometimes surrounded by a palisade of oak, and outside the aurla there was a level green called* ***faithche*** *(fauha), which was used for athletic games; also called* ***blai.*** *This green extended as far as the crowing of a cock or the sound of a bell would carry. It was free to all-comers. Many raths contained underground chambers of a beehive construction: according to Dr. Sigerson there were ten thousand rath-caves in the south and west of Ireland. Those underground chambers were used in times of peace as storehouses, and in time of war as places of refuge for women and children. In the residence of a* ***bo-aire,*** *or well-to-do farmer, at least seven dwellings were contained within the lis; the dwelling house, kitchen at the back of house and pigsty. Those houses were all separate buildings on the same plan as the rath. The sunniest part of the house called the* ***grianan*** *(greenaun) was set-aside for women and children.*

In the large raths, a special room was provided, which was called the House of Conversation; in this room, the family sat and received visitors. In after times during the struggles of the Irish against the invaders, outlawed persons took refuge in the rath-caves, from whence may have arisen the legends of voices and singing heard underground in the fort, always attributed to the "good people". These raths are found in Scotland and throughout Europe – they were in use in Scotland down to the eighteenth century. The Irish rath was the home of the Irish people from the days of the Firbolgs for nearly three thousand years.

Some idea of life in an Irish rath of the better class can be gathered from the following descriptions, which are taken from Mrs Green's History. A poem of Teigue Dall O'Higgins, *spoke of the reign of Elizabeth, 1581:*

"One night I came to ***Eas Caoille****; to the Judgement Day shall I think of it; our visit to that dwelling shall abide forever; the manner of the night, and what were each one's doing there. The like of those men, that in that rath, perfected with the freshest hue, I found waiting for me, ranged along the walls of the be-crimsoned mansion, before themselves no eyes had seen. Midway down one side of the hall, Maolmora sat, and among the great concourse of bards there sat by him; the poet-in-chief of Turlough O'Neill, of Mac William Bourke of Clanrickard. They stood up beside the host and pledged him in ale, quaffed from golden goblets and from beakers of horn; and before they slept*

Teigue told his story for a price and took his gifts of honour; from Maolmora a dappled horse, from O'Neill's bard, a wolf-dog, from him of Clanrickard a little book that was a well brimful of the stream of knowledge; it was the flower of Ireland's royal books, and, from the bard of Mac William Bourke his harp – a harp of the minstrel-in-chief of the Bourke's blood; and there it is as good as ever, but he that gave it is not here.'" This was one of the last meetings of the Irish bards who met in the house of Maolmora McSwiney, "A house white and fair." At this time the bards were doomed!

The dun was the rath of an Irish King, and the dress of an Irish King is given as follows:- *"A scarlet tunic and gold-edged coat, a saffron-coloured belt; buckles with crystal and gold tassels; a white-embroidered hood; armour gilt in delicate patterns, and a conical helmet inlaid with gold branches, and sitting beside him his chief Brehon and chief Ollave."*

The Ollaves were the most highly educated of the professional classes, corresponding to our degree of Doctor.

In the banquets of the duns or palaces, the guests sat at a table each according to his rank under his shield, which was hung on the wall of the banquet-hall over the place where the guest sat. The main drinks before the year 1405 A.D. were ale, mead and wine, while after the year 1405 usquebaugh, Irish uisce beatha (ishke-baha), water-of-life, or whiskey. The wine was imported in exchange for hides. Ale was the ordinary drink, and was made from honey and was much esteemed. A kind of cider was made from wild crab apples and bilberries (known as froghans), which grow on the mountain.

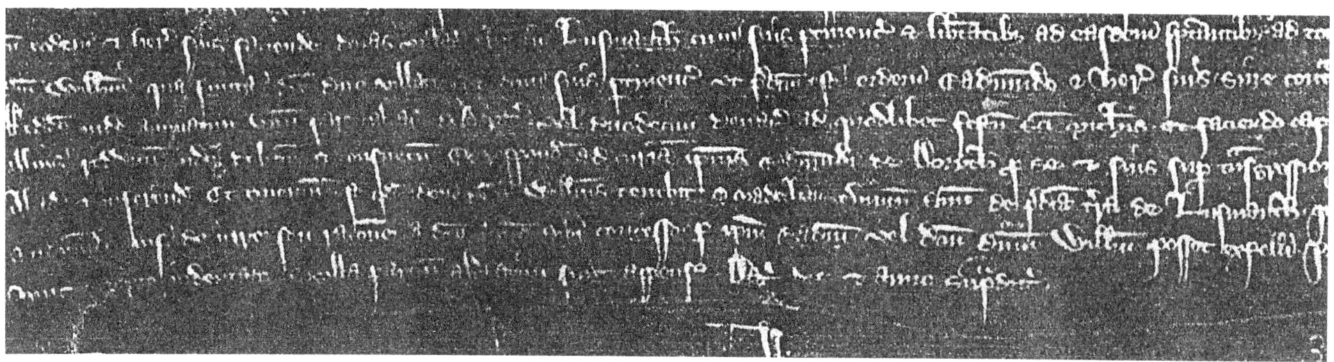

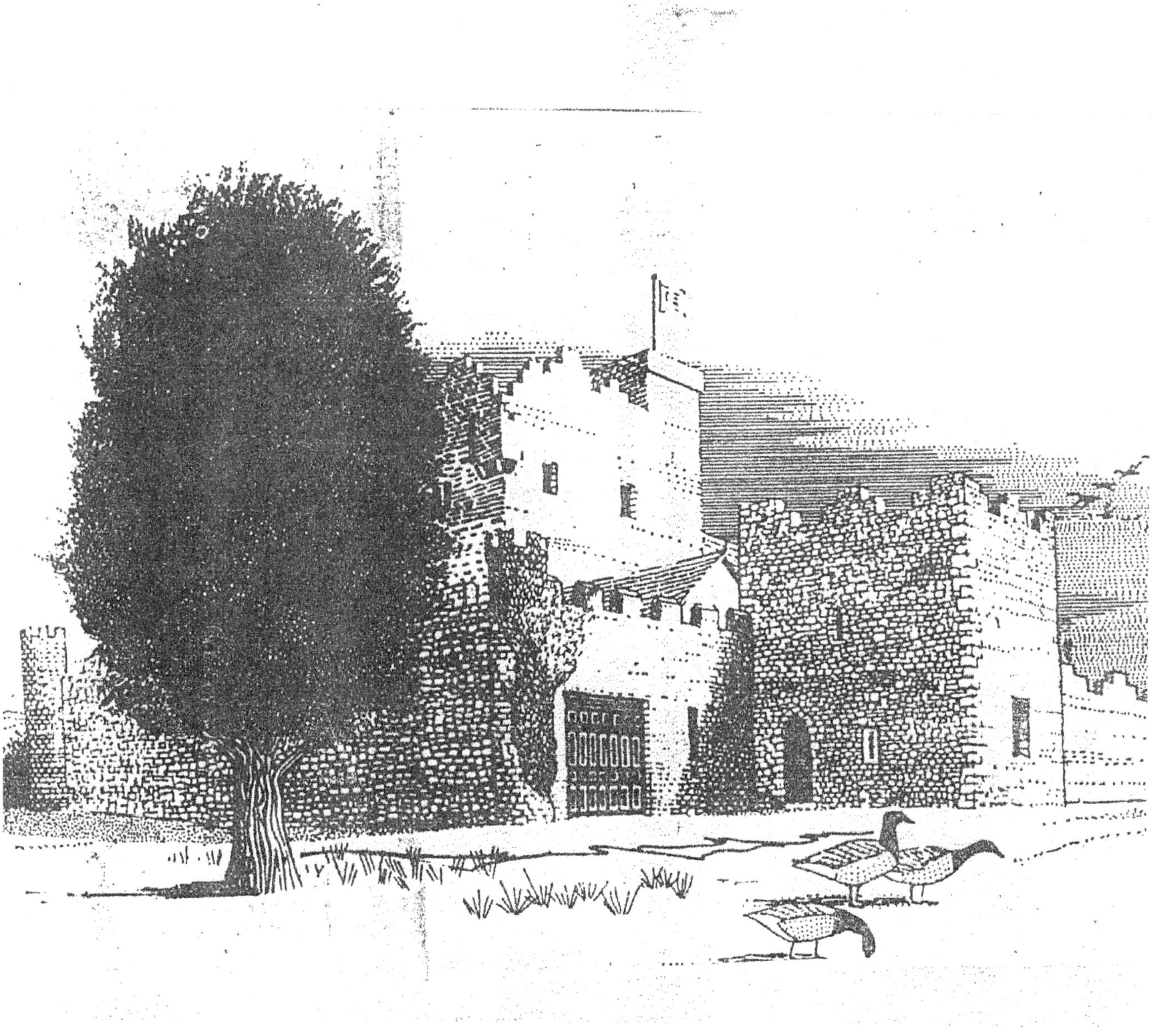

Medieval deed referring to Lusmagh, dated 1308

Chapter 4

Celtic Twilight – The O'Maddens and De Burgos and the Non-Existent Destruction in 1557

CELTIC TWILIGHT

The O'Maddens and De Burgos and the Non-Existent Destruction in 1557

To try to discover what actually happened at Cloghan between 1204 and 1595, we have to turn to the family trees of the O'Maddens and the De Burgos (who later became the Earls of Clanrickarde).

The MacCoughlans owned land in Lusmagh right up to the later eighteenth century, indeed one family is still there and has been for many centuries, but their family tree is not well documented. Their power and position had been badly eroded over the centuries. In the 17th century, they were almost extinguished by Plantation and the trouble caused to them by The Crown through Mathew De Renzi, owner of Clonony Castle. De Renzi's extensive correspondence still exists.

It is probable that the MacCoughlans held Lusmagh in its entirety at some stage or another, but there is no proof of it that I can find. The fortunes of the Clanrickardes and O'Maddens are easier to research and the two families were very much intertwined by marriage, war and alliance.

The Normans did not hold Lusmagh for long according to George Cunningham in his book *Anglo-Normanan advance into the South West Midlands of Ireland 1185 – 1221*. But we do know they were here in 1308 from a Norman document about *Delusmagh*. I believe that the Norman Butlers of Ormonde controlled Lusmagh until they were defeated twice in battles by Eoghan O'Madden in 1336. According to the O'Madden family tree, it looks very likely that the O'Madden who took over from them was the son of Murchadh O'Madden, Chief of Sil Anmchadha, who was known as Murchadh of 'Magh Bealaigh' (which means 'a strong castle') and Murchadh 'of proud voice'.

Murchadh went overseas with De Burgo, not only on a pilgrimage to Rome but to also join the 8th Crusade with the contingent leaving with Prince Edward of England. Murchadh came back to Ireland but later relinquished his chieftainship in order to return to Rome where he was buried in St. Peter's. It is thought that with him the O'Madden crest and coat of arms were achieved. His son Eoghan was born in 1260.

Eoghan was thought to have gone abroad, whilst a young boy, with his father. He became Chief in 1318 and remained so for 25 years until 1347. Eoghan was known variously as 'The Great O'Madden', 'Lion of Birra', and 'The Fine Hazel Nut of Aughrim'. He is described, in a poem of that day as: *A man with the courage of a true lion, the Lion of Birra, with the venom of the serpent, the Hawk of the Shannon, a tower which defends the frontiers, a Griffin of the race of Con of the Hundred Battles, a large man of slender body, with skin like the blossom of the apple trees, with brown eyebrows, black curling hair, long fingers and a cheek like the cherries.'* In his youth, Eoghan was against the English interest in Connaught. In 1306, although married to Melissa the daughter of Redmond de Burgo, Eoghan defeated the Earl of Ulster, also a De Burgo, killing sixty-six of De Burgo's people.

Later though, upon the arrival of Edward Bruce from Scotland in 1315, Eoghan joined with the De Burgos against Ladky O'Kelly who was Chief of Hy Many and Rory O'Connor who was presumptive King of Connaught and all the supporters of Bruce. Through the manoeuvres of a grateful, or perhaps wise, De Burgo, and through the Justicar for the Crown, (called Mortimer), the Earl of Ulster ensured that Eoghan and his heirs were granted priority by the English Crown.

It was said that Eoghan 'built a strong castle of stone and wood' and his wife was described by a Bard, *'of fair hair and curling tresses, the noblest woman he had seen in his time'.*

Eoghan died in 1347 at the age of 87. He is my candidate for the title, Builder, or, Re-builder, of Cloghan Castle. Eoghan's eldest son was slain by the De Burgos in 1340 and his second son Murchadh was Chief from 1347 – 1371. One has to admit that in those days a family quarrel was a pretty drastic thing!

Murchadh was noted as a generous patron of the literati, the poor and the needy of Ireland, he was killed by one shot of an arrow in the rear of a predatory party in Ormonde, (the lands to the south of Lusmagh now in Tipperary). Murchadh's daughter, Lady More, married Richard MacWilliam Burke, also a De Burgo. Their son became the first Earl of Clanrickarde. Lady More died in 1383 of the great plague.

These De Burgos lived as Irish Chieftains. They obeyed Brehon Law, practised fosterage of the children, gossiprey, coyne and livery and spoke the Irish language. They ruled their territory as Chiefs until the reign of King Henry VIII. In their appearance, they let their hair grow, dyed their shirts yellow by using valuable saffron and favoured large sleeves and short tunics.

They covered their outfits with rough cloaks. These were hairy on the outside, lined on the inside, generously proportioned and extremely warm. The cloaks became a protection against sword cuts and by wrapping themselves up in them, the Irish were able to sleep in the open in all weathers. We can assume these cloaks were indeed effective, as English authorities later banned them as Weapons of War. Today, we can see the remains of the original design in the Clonakilty Cloak. In 1950, whilst hitch-hiking around Ireland, I saw the ladies in Clonakilty still wearing these voluminous, hooded cloaks which today are reproduced in silk and wool for evening wear. The ones I saw were heirlooms passed down from earlier generations, all black on the outside and beautifully quilted inside.

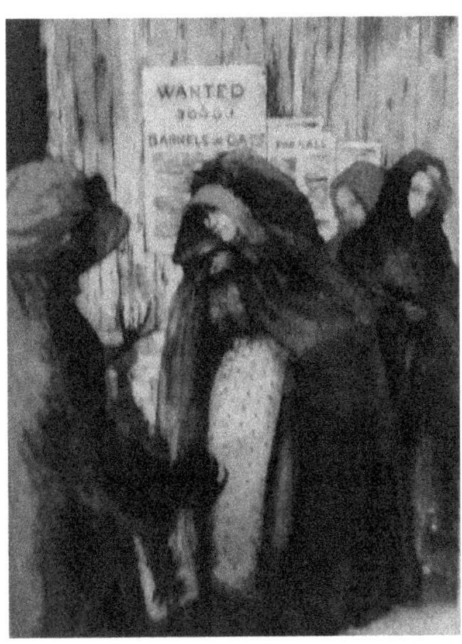

Clonakilty Cloaks: a drawing from from the 1930s by Brian's artist cousin, the late Amy O'Donovan

In 1411, Morogh O'Madden succeeded as Chief. He was said in some pedigrees to have been the founder of Meelick Abbey. Morogh died in 1451. Others say the Abbey was built twenty years later. His grandson – Morogh Reagh O'Madden – succeeded to the Chieftainship on the death of his father Eoghan, for whom no dates are recorded. Morogh Reagh had five sons, two of whom were slain in 1486. His younger son Murchadh had a very beautiful daughter who married Richard Burke, as the De Burgo's were now called, in 1519 and took with her all the Portumna lands and estates. This aroused great fury amongst the O'Madden Clan. So much fury in fact that for the next three generations, these two intertwined families slaughtered each other to an appalling degree – brother against brother, cousin against cousin. This pitiful story occurred in other clans at the same time, as told in the records of the O'Carrolls, and the MacCoughlans.

In 1556 John and Mealeachlainn Modarda O'Madden were each made chiefs of half the O'Madden territory. Mealeachlainn Modarda ruled as full Chief after his brother had killed John O'Madden and he remained chief until 1567. This Mealeachlainn Modarda O'Madden lived in Cloghan Castle, Lusmagh. This is when the castle must have been a hive of activity – soldiers, servants, cooks, horsemen and bards etc, etc.

In 1557, Mealeachlainn Balb O'Madden was taken from his castle at Meelick by the Chief Justice after a siege. When in July 1557, the English in Athlone floated huge cannons down the River Shannon to Meelick and bombarded and ruined the O'Madden castle, they then asked the way to Cloghan Castle and were obviously 'helped' by an O'Madden who directed them to Cloghan Castle in the village of Cloghan. *This* Cloghan Castle was, however, a MacCoughlan castle. The official records of the time recorded the destruction of Cloghan Castle in Lusmagh but it was the wrong Cloghan Castle! To this day, official government publications state that our Cloghan Castle was destroyed in 1557 and later rebuilt. This is nonsense.

The pressures were on the family from every direction as the English crown and its employees were wiping out the old Celtic way of life. Donnell O'Madden, nephew of Mealeachlainn Modarda was the last Chief of Siol Anmchada who ruled the territory according to the old Irish system. He was regarded as a powerful, brave warrior. He was the most celebrated Chieftain since the death of Eoghan in 1347. He and his son Ambrose (who later died in Cloghan Castle), had a dramatic and narrow escape from death as told in *The legend of Meelick:*

> *"In the year 1577, memorable in Irish annals for the Massacre of Mullaghmast, Donal O'Madden, Chieftain of Silanchia, together with his son Ambrose, set forth from their Castle of Lismore, between Eyrecourt and Meelick to meet some of his kinsmen from another of his strongholds on the opposite side of the Shannon, viz – Cloghan Castle, who were to accompany them to a gathering at Mullaghmast in Kildare to which all the still unconquered Irish Chieftains were invited by the English Deputy, Sir Henry Sydney. They were there to ratify a solemn pact or Treaty of Peace between the native sects and their invaders.*
>
> *It was the twilight hour of a lovely evening when the travellers started from Lismore Castle situated near Meelick Abbey, and as they rode along they heard the vesper bell of the Abbey calling the monks to prayer. For a brief moment, they halted at the gates, then passed onwards towards Cloghan Castle – all save two – the chieftain, Donnell O'Madden, and his heir, Ambrose, who, as the Abbey bell chimed, exclaimed* – "Hark! The Monks of Meelick are about to chant a requiem over the departed of our race in yonder tombs, and shall we pass heedlessly on our way?"
>
> *The Lord of Silanchia of that day, who, if we may judge from his history, was evidently more of a warrior than of a saint, reluctantly complied with the youth's request, saying* – "Thy pious wishes, my son, are somewhat ill-timed, nevertheless they shall not be thwarted although we will have to ride all the faster on our long journey to Offalia." *They dismounted and entered the Abbey gates, and remained until the last notes of the solemn melody had resounded through the aisles of the Abbey, when they resumed their way through the trees that then extended between the monastery and the Shannon. Scarcely had they done so, when the young chieftain's horse stood still and would proceed no further as if suddenly arrested by some hand invisible in the gloom of the night. "Who dares to stay my horse? Allow me to pass," Ambrose angrily exclaimed. As he spoke he beheld a tall phantom figure, upon which the moonbeams faintly glimmered through the overhanging trees of the wood, and shrank back affrighted, while listening to the words of the spectre:*
>
> "Wherefore feel alarm? From yonder tomb I come to warn of an impending doom! Long years have passed away since thine ancestor, Eoghan O'Madden, was numbered with the dead. A proud and bloodstained warrior, alas! I lived and died yet not unshriven, not unforgiven, but unfit for heaven. That vesper prayer, in which thou, my descendant, didst share, hath reached my prison home, and soon will my long penance end. Thou, who for the forgotten

dead didst pray, I haste to warn on thy way and bid thee and thine venture not near the Rath of Mullaghmast. The guests who gather, when sinks the sun in the west, shall when again the sun glows in the east, be as I am now."

The strange words ceased, and the spectral form disappeared. Then the awe-stricken listener related all to his astonished father, Donnell O'Madden, who returned with his son to Meelick, and remained for the night at the monastery, too deeply impressed by the warning of the unearthly visitant to doubt of its fulfilment or to proceed on their journey to Offaly. Within a week came the tidings of the fate of the guests at the Rath of Mullaghmast – how, during the meeting, it was surrounded by the soldiery who at their chief's command rushed in and put to death more than four hundred unsuspecting guests. It is a historical fact that of the 400 chiefs and the followers assembled in the house at that time, not one escaped massacre by the forces of Sir Henry Sydney.

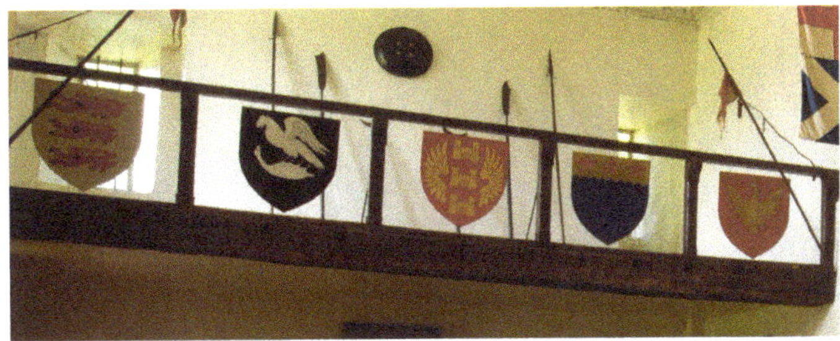

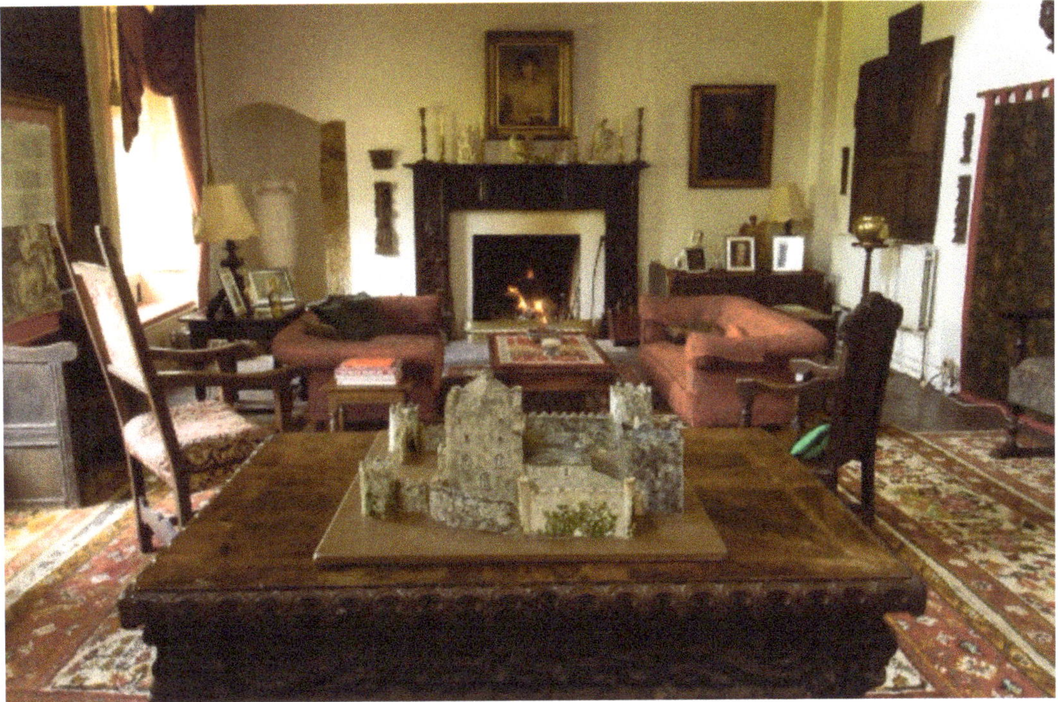

The four shields of the major families to have lived at Cloghan ©Tina Claffey

Chapter 5

The 1595 Siege

The 1595 Siege

THE END OF THE CELTIC WAY OF LIFE

In one way this book is all about power:

The power of the Monasteries

The power of the Irish Clan Chiefs

The power of the Norman invaders

The power of the Norman and Gaelic Overlords

The power of the English Crown

The power of the Roman Catholic Church

The power of the Irish Politicians, in particular, Fianna Fail, who I call "The Farmers Party"

The power of Money

In 1595 the rule of the O'Madden Clan in Lusmagh at Cloghan Castle came to an abrupt end:

THE SIEGE

Donnell O'Madden was the last chief of Siol Anmchadha. Here follows an extract from *'Tribes and Customs of Hy Many.'*

"In 1585, according to the Annals of the Four Masters, O'Madden attended the parliament convened at Dublin, to which the Irish chieftains who were obedient to the Queen were summoned, but in 1595 we find him in open rebellion. In that year, Cloghan, one of his castles in the district or parish of Lusmagh, on the east side of the Shannon, was summoned to surrender to the Lord Deputy, Sir William Russell, but O'Madden's people replied that they would not surrender even though all the soldiers were Deputies. This famous reply of O'Madden's people is referred to by Brewer in his *Beauties of Ireland,* Vol. II Pg. 152, and, as the Editor has heard many express their doubt of its authenticity, he is tempted to give here the whole account of the transaction from Sir William Russell's Journal, which he has procured through the kindness of Sir Frederic Madden, of the British Museum. The following extract is from the Journal of Sir William Russell, Lord Deputy of Ireland, preserved in MS. Add. 4728. Brit. Museum. To which Institution it was presented by Lord Willoughby, of Parham, 18th May 1764-Fol. 61 b.:'

"Thursdaie 11 (March 1595)'. From Rathingelduld my Lord rode to Cloghan, O'Madden's Castle, in Losmage (now Lusmagh). Before we encamped, in cominge to wch we passed through a straight pace (pass) of 4 miles in lenth. O'Madden himself beinge gone out in action of Rebellion, and had left a ward of his principle men in his Castle, whoe as soone as they perceived my Lord to approach neare, they sett three of their houses on fire, adjoining to the Castle, and made shott at us out of the Castle, wich hurt two of our souldiers and a boye. And beinge sent to by my Lord to yield upp the Castle to the Queene, their answere was to Capten Tho. Lee that if all that came in his L (sic) Companie were Deputies, they would not yield, but said they would trust to the strength of their Castle, and hoped by to morrowe that time that the Deputie and his Companie should stand in as great feare, as they then were, in expectinge, as it should seeme, some ayde to relieve them. That night my Lord appointed Cap. Izod to keepe a sure watch aboute the said Castle, for that a mayne bogg was adioyneing there unto, and appointed the kearne with certain souldiers to watch theire, least they should make an attempt to escape that way. About midnight my L. visited the watch, and understanding of some women to be within the Castle, sent to them againe, and advised them to put forth their women, for that hee intended the next morninge to assault the Castle with fire and sword, but they refused soe to doe, and would not suffer their women to come forth.

"Fridae 12.' My L. continued before the Castle, and as preparation was making for fire works, to fire the Castle, one in Sr. Wm. Clarke's Companie beinge nere the Castle, by making tryall cast vpp a fire brand to the top of the roufe which was covered with thatch, and presentlie tooke fire, and burned the roufe, which greatlie dismaide them, where upon the alarm was stroke up, and whilst our shott plaied at their spike holes, a fire was made to the grate and the doore, which smothered manie of them, and which all the souldiers made a breach in the wall and entered the Castle, and took manie of them alive, most of which were cast over the walles, and soe executed. And soe the whole number which were burned and kild in the Castle were fortie and six persons, besides two women and a boye, which were saved by my Lord's appointment.

Fol. 64 – 'The names of such cheife men as were kilde in the Castle of Cloghan O'Madden, at ye wininge thereof, which were principall fightinge men, the xii of March 1595.

Shane McBrasill O'Madden of Corlogher, gent.

Cahill McShane O'Madden of Kineghan, gent.

Donnogh McO'Madden of Tomhaligh, gent.

Owen McShane O'Madden of the same, gent.

Molaghlin Duffe McColeghan of Ballymacoleghan, gent. Captain of shott, and his two sonnes.

Shane McKygan, a shott.

Tho. Bey of Hanyne, a shott.

William Dolland, a shott.

Mortaugh O'Kenny, a shott.

Manose Oge O'Kryan, of O'Rorcke's Countrie, Captain of shott, and O'Rourke's mother's brother's sonne.

Shane Enemeny O'Connor, of the Countie of Sligo, gent. Who said when hee was taken, he was a good prisoner to bee ransomed.

More, two other gent. Of O'Rorke's Country, whose names were not knowne.

The names of the Cheife men kild in the Conflict the daie before the wyninge of the Castle, viz:

Ambrose McMolaghline Mottere O'Madden of Clare Maden, gent.

Coheghe Oge O'Madden of the same, gent.

Leve O'Madden of Clare, gent. Three landed men.

Leve O'Conner of y'Countie of Sligo, a cheife gent & a leader of shott and Scotts; he was buried at Meelicke.

Ferdoregh McEverye, a Cap. Of Scotts.

Ever McGarell, of Galry, gent.

McConnell, chiefe of the Scotts.

Vlicke Bowrcke McEdmond Bowrcke of Balyely, gent.

The rest were shott, bowmen and kearne, the whole number kild & drown'd (besides those in the Castle) were seaven score and upwards, besides some hurt, were escaped, beinge unarmed and fled in greate amasement.'

It does not appear that for these daring deeds O'Madden's property was confiscated, for we find him "loyal again" in 1602, when he attacked the magnificent rebel, Donell O'Sullivan Beare, who, after the defeat of the Irish at Kinsale, and the taking of his castle of Dunboy, was passing through Siol – Anmchadha, on his way to O'Rourke. O'Madden was evidently pardoned by James I and we find that on the 8th March 1611, he settled his property on his sons according to the laws of England, as appears by a deed (9Jac. I Roll 2), whereby Donell O'Madden of Longford, in the county of Galway, captain of his nation, granted to feoffees (seize…sic) his Manor and Castle of Longford and all other property in the county of Galway to hold to the use of Ambrose, otherwise Anmaha O'Madden, son and heir of the said Donell and the heirs male of his body, remainder to his (the grantor's) sons Malachy and Donell and their respective heirs male, remainder to Brasil O'Madden, son of Hugh O'Madden one of the sons of the said Donell O'Madden, and his heirs male, remainder to the heirs (general) of Ambrose O'Madden forever.

Captain Lee's men successfully set fire to the castle's thatched roof, 46 soldiers were piked off the battlements, while women and children escaped through the, now defunct, underground tunnel. It should be mentioned in all fairness to the representatives of the Crown, who come out of the story in an unflattering light, that the O'Maddens, Scot's Mercenaries and friends, had been out on the rampage looting and burning other people's homes! That is why they were pursued to Cloghan Castle with a contingent of Molloys and MacCoughlans in the besieging party.

In the Elizabethan State Paper 47, dated 20 March 1595, by John Lye to Sir Geof. Fenton, we read:

'O'Maddens Castle of Cloghan here betwixt 2 rivers in Lusmagh and upon the edge of the Shannon and in the strongest place in Ireland which was fortified in such sort as the ward thought themselves safe against all men uttering great words, that they did not care a rush for my Lord Deputy and all his forces. But my Lord Deputy most honourably and courageously went in the face of the enemies, shot and beset the castle on every side so that in the end it was most honourably won after 2 days and 2 nights siege. The men of the ward put to sword and burned from the defaced castle of Cloghan.'

The O'Maddens took up their other properties, but the 245 years of ownership of Cloghan Castle had ended. The crown took Cloghan Castle and its lands in Lusmagh in 1595. The O'Maddens then built Derryhinney Castle near Portumna – the last castle tower house built in Ireland.

In 1601, Queen Elizabeth granted Cloghan Castle and its 6,000 acres to Sir John Moore.

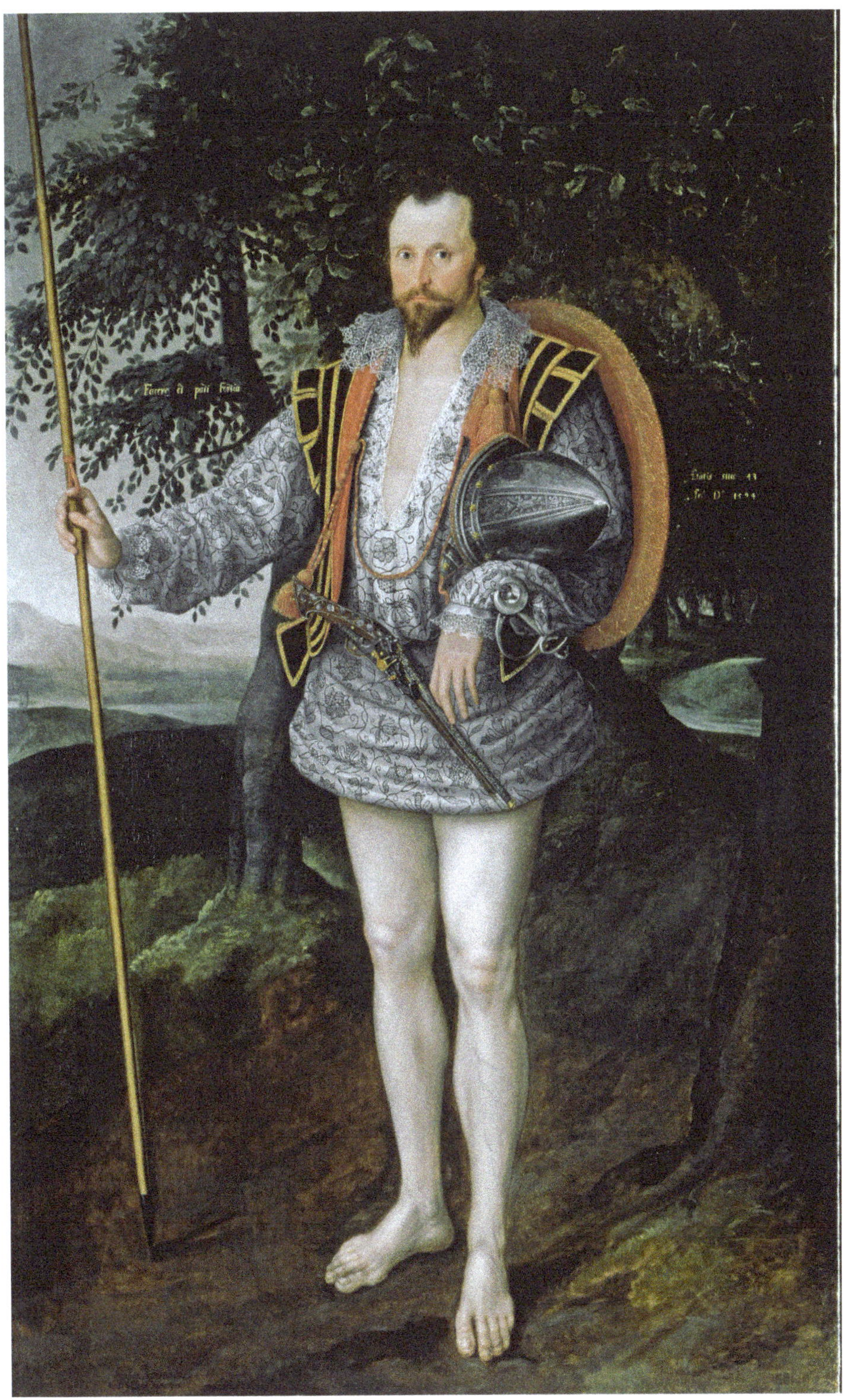

Portrait of Captain Thomas Lee, 1594, Marcus Gheeraerts II (1561 - 1636) with kind permission from Tate Britain. This is the oldest painting in their collection. It is well worth reading about this painting's fascinating iconography, and there are various online resources by the Tate and other historians. Suffice to say, the effort undertaken by Captain Lee to display his loyalty to his Queen was sadly to no avail: he was later executed for treason.

Chapter 6

Anglo-Norman Irish, The Moores of Barmeath and The Victoria Crosses

The Anglo-Norman Irish, The Moores of Barmeath and The Victoria Crosses

Barmeath is one of the oldest inhabited castles in Ireland and it sits on gently sloping ground overlooking the Irish Sea and the Mourne Mountains, in County Louth. It is now, and has been for hundreds of years, the family home of Lord and Lady Bellew.

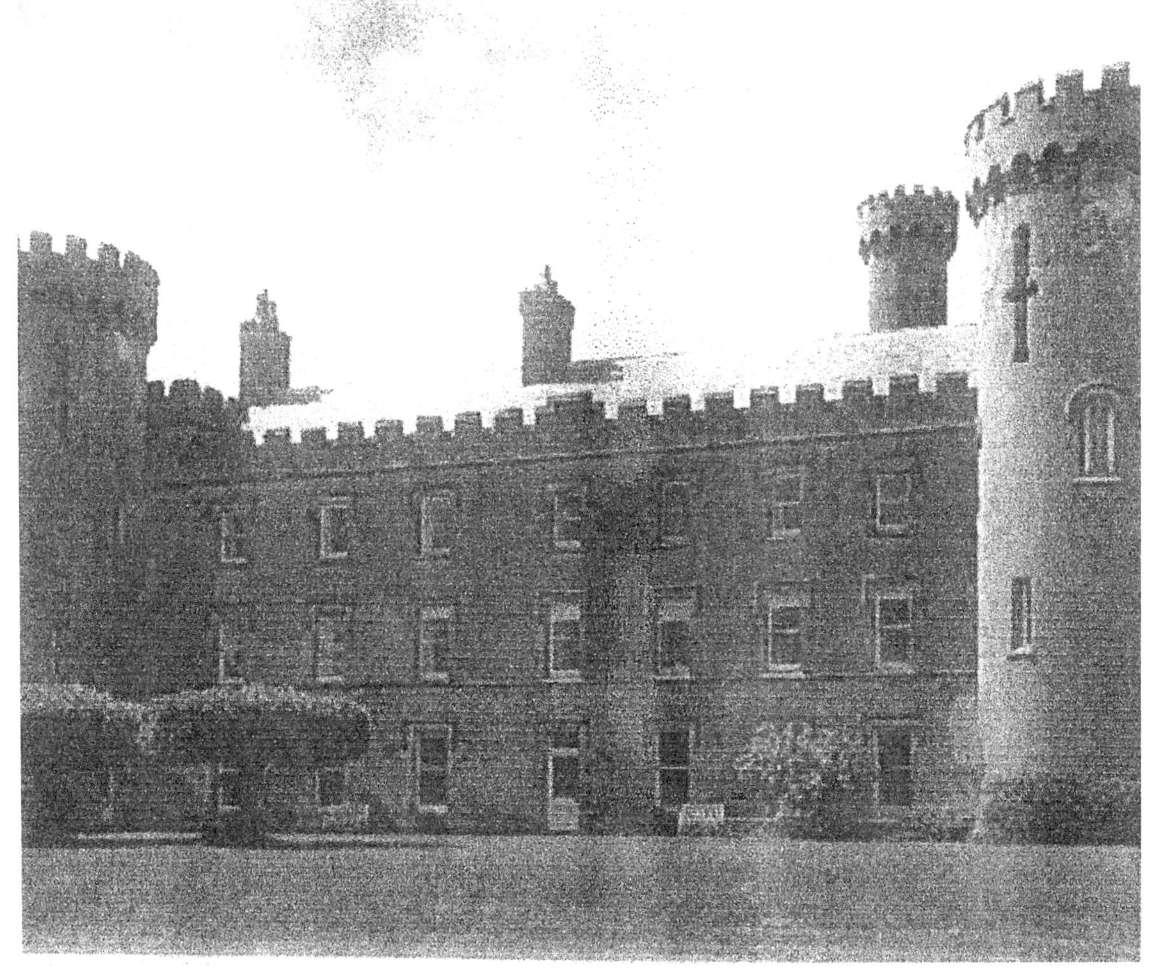

Barmeath Castle

The Moores have been traced back over a thousand years to Norway from where they went to Normandy. They followed William the Conqueror to England and settled in the County of Kent. They then moved to County Louth in the 12th Century and settled in Barmeath Castle, which they lost in the Cromwellian confiscations.

The Moores were remarkable by any standards and have attracted the attention of one University Lecturer who followed their careers in County Mayo, a Cork University Professor who made a major study of them and their pedigree, and an American Moore with a degree in history who traced their origin back beyond Normandy. It is said that Saint Sir Thomas Moore was of the Barmeath family and it is very likely that the writer George Moore from County Mayo was also one of them.

They were superb horsemen and one of them won the Aintree Grand National as an amateur jockey. Many of them became lawyers and married into famous families. They became very wealthy but lost it all in 1854. Descendants live in Australia, Ireland, England, USA and possibly France. Families can be well known for their titles, careers in the public eye or for academic achievements – the Moores had much, much, more! Their main claim to fame is so beyond normal comprehension that I feel that it requires a very full explanation. They were brave beyond belief. The Victoria Cross is probably the most difficult award for courage that can be earned. It is a mark of such distinction that servicemen hold it in awe worldwide. The Barmouth Moores did not have one V.C. in the family – *they had three!* Their medals for bravery included a few Military Crosses also. This is not just bravery, it is almost superhuman.

THE VICTORIA CROSS

29th January 1856 was the date that the Victoria Cross was instituted by order of Queen Victoria. It was to be awarded for an act of extreme bravery or heroism in times of war. In the first 150 years of its existence, millions of men and women served in the armed forces of the British Empire. However, during that time, in countless wars around the world, only 1,350 were awarded.

The Victoria Cross is regarded with veneration. Generals will salute Privates wearing it. Statues are erected of men who were awarded it. It is the award to the "Bravest of the Brave". It is probably the most highly rated and respected medal in the world. An extraordinarily disproportionate number of those V.C.'s were awarded to Irishmen for acts of outstanding bravery.

The Moore family came from Normandy to County Louth eight hundred years ago and in 1601 a descendant of the family settled in Cloghan Castle. Some of them changed their names to O'Moore – in the mid-eighteenth century.

Arthur Thomas Moore (later Major General) was born in Carlingford, County Louth in 1830. He was awarded the V.C. in 1857 in Persia. *"Lt Moore charged an infantry square of 500 Persians at the head of his regiment, jumped his horse over the bayonets of the enemy and stood over his dead horse with a shattered sabre. With a fellow officer, he fought his way out of the square."* This V.C. was sold at auction in 2004 and fetched £172,500, the second-highest price ever paid for a V.C.

Hans Garrett Moore was the son of Captain Garrett Moore of the 88th Regiment, The Connaught Rangers, of the Moore family of Cloghan Castle. He was educated at The Royal School, Banagher and Trinity College, Dublin. In 1855, he obtained a commission without purchase on account of his family's distinguished service to the Crown in the Crimea. He served in India during the mutiny and was eventually posted to South Africa when he fought in the Zulu Wars. In 1877, Major Moore commanded a patrol of Connaught Rangers accompanied by mounted police who were attacked by a column of 1,000 foot and 600 mounted Zulu's. His incredible bravery in this action, when his horse was shot from under him, won him the V.C.

Major Garrett O'Moore Creagh – whose mother was born in Cloghan Castle - was born in 1848. He rose to the rank of Major General, was knighted and was Commander of the British Army in India from 1909-1914. He was a captain in the Bombay Staff Corps in India at the outbreak of the Afghan War. The Merwara Battalion volunteered for service in that war and Captain Creagh was the only European Officer in it.

In April 1879, Captain Creagh was sent with 150 men to protect the village of Kamdake on the Cabul River. 1,500 men, who commanded the heights above them, attacked Kamdake and Captain Creagh's 150 soldiers. His forces took up a defensive position in a cemetery and *"held out against the enemy repeatedly and often with bayonets, being ultimately relieved by the Bengal Lancers".* For this action, he was awarded the Victoria Cross.

In his later service, he was mentioned in Despatches no fewer than five times. He served 48 years in the army and became ADC General to HM the King. His son was a Brigade Major of the Hussars who won the Military Cross in World War One.

Extracts from *"History of the Victoria Cross"*, by Philip A. Wilkins.

> **MOORE, HANS GARRETT:**Lieutenant Moore served with his regiment in the Indian Mutiny Campaign from December 1857, including the affair of Bhognapore, the siege of Lucknow in March, the siege of Calpee, action of Selimpore (slightly wounded) and Jamoo, storming and capture of the Birwah Forts (slightly wounded). It is said by an old comrade that *"at Selimpore the 88s were shot off his forage-cap, and at Birwah his revolver broken at his side, while in the same action he made a furious onslaught alone on a party of three of the enemy in a native house, the result of which we should never have known from him had we not, on missing him, ascertained that, armed only with his regulation sword, he had disposed of the party single-handed. Yet to show what a chivalrous nature was his, I saw him not long afterwards risk his own life to save a poor native coolie, who was one of our beaters in a shooting party in Oudh, and who, on missing his footing and falling into the Goomti River, them in rapid flood, was rescued by Moore at once plunging in, clothes and all, and bringing him almost lifeless to the bank. Would to heaven that help as effectual had been near him when his own gallant life was taken in the same element."*

It further reads:

"At the time of his death a brother officer wrote to a newspaper: "Many of your military readers learned with regret of the untimely death of Colonel Hans Garrett Moore, V.C. – 'Bould Moore', as he was called by the men of his old regiment, The Connaught Rangers. A more intrepid soldier never lived. I remember during the last Kaffir War, when he was wounded trying to save a man who had fallen into the hands of the Kaffirs, and for which he got the V.C When the doctor was trying to take the bent assegai-head out of his arm, some anxious bystander attempted to cut open the sleeve of his patrol jacket, when, with perfect coolness, he said, 'Hold on, this is my only coat; rip it up the seam.' The next morning he went out to look for the Kaffirs, and found them twenty to one, and after three hours fighting, defeated them. He was the only officer who rode his horse out of action, all the other having been killed or captured. He said to me, 'Where is my horse wounded?' and on examination I found three distinct bullets had entered, but the poor animal carried him home that night and then died." At the time of Colonel Moore's death the following letter, giving an account of the second action at Draaibosch, appeared in the "Cape Times":

Cape Town, 18 Nov. 1889. To the Editor of the Cape Times:

"Sir, the brief notice that has appeared in the newspapers respecting that gallant soldier, Colonel Moore, whose untimely death is so deplored, has been supplemented by a letter written to the 'Irish Times' by an old Connaught Ranger, in which he bears testimony (were testimony needed) to the splendid qualities of the deceased officer, whom he rightly terms 'as intrepid a soldier as ever lived.' The writer mentioned that Colonel Moore admitted to him that he 'was in a funk' on one occasion and that was in the action at Draaibosch, on the 30th Dec. 1877. May I, as one who had the privilege of serving with Colonel Moore on that day, tell your readers in what kind of a way that 'funk' displayed itself. Our men, some fifty of the Connaught Rangers, about thirty of the F.A.M. Police (who were dismounted for the action), and five or six volunteers, were in line on the crest of the hill above the Draaibosch Hotel and facing the Komgha Road, towards which, and from the direction of Sandilli's Kraal, on the banks of the Kabousie, the whole force of the enemy, some 1,000 foot and 600 horse, were advancing. Suddenly, and when within about 350 yards of us, they deployed, one half sweeping round to our left flank, and the remainder to our right, whilst the horse went at a canter to our rear. It was a critical moment. Colonel Moore, who was mounted, told Capt. Acklom to move the men at the double to the crest of the hill, facing Savage's Shop, as the force of the enemy flanking our position in that direction were nearest, and were then charging up the hill with loud cries. Before the movement could be completed the enemy were upon us – some of the F.A.M. Police flung themselves on their horses and rode hard away (I may mention that others of that force remained and did gallant service afterwards), and the young soldiers of the Rangers, mere boys for

the most part, showed signs of wavering. What, at this moment, was Colonel Moore doing? He was sitting immovably, calm, on his horse, facing the hordes of the enemy, and issuing the words of the command to his forces as if he had been on parade. One indecision on his part even, I verily believe, had he turned his horse's head from the enemy and our little force would have been annihilated. But there he was: there his young soldiers saw him, the grim, stern personification of the warrior undaunted in the very face of what to all seemed certain death. And the men in a moment reassured, halted at the entreaties of their officers, and with ringing cheers charged with the bayonet, and for the moment checked the rush of the savages. Colonel Moore throughout the day (on which he held the hill to his last cartridge, and during which he had his horse three times shot under him) displayed the same perfect coolness and calm courage, and by those qualities, I am persuaded saved the Colony from the devastation which would have followed a defeat of his force in that first and the most remarkable action of the campaign, an action in which, moreover, the natives for the first and only time in their history, charged our soldiers to the very point of the bayonet. Remember, too, that only thirty-six hours previously Colonel Moore had been dangerously wounded by an assegai whilst endeavouring to protect the body of Private Giese against a horde of assailants. This was the 'funk' displayed by Colonel Moore on the one occasion on which he owned to it.

I am, etc, W.J.J.W."

The Eastern Province Herald, of 29 Jan. 1877, says; "It is to the engagement of the 30th Dec. that we wish to direct special attention. On that day, Major Moore, though severely wounded by an assegai on the previous day, left Komgha with forty men of the 88th Regt., under Capt. Acklom, and twenty-one men of the F.A.M. Police, under Sub-Inspector White, for the purpose of escorting the mail from the Transkei past Draaibosch, the post riders of the previous day having made three unsuccessful attempts to carry it through to Gray's Farm. As this small party of sixty-one men, and three or four others who went as volunteers, approached Savager's Shop, about six miles from Komgha, the enemy was seen to be collecting in force and forming an attack. Major Moore selected a good defensive position on the crown of a hill about half a mile beyond Savage's Shop and close to the road, and now began a fight which lasted an hour and a half, such as is rarely seen in Kaffir warfare, in which frequent bayonet charges; were made by the colonial forces. It is seldom, indeed, that Kaffirs give them the chance, and the only matter for regret in this instance is that the defensive force did not consist of older and more experienced men. The forty men of the 88th Regt. – The Connaught Rangers – we are told, were mere boys, 'not one of whom had ever seen an enemy before, and their firing was wild.' Their courage is not questioned for a moment, and they charged with a cheer when called upon, every time repulsing the enemy… . It is a wonder that this small force, under such circumstances, was not completely cut up. The bayonet charges, no doubt, were their salvation… . The fight lasted from 2.15 p.m. to 3.45 p.m., say an hour and a half." For his services in this campaign, Brevet Major H. G. Moore was mentioned in Despatches (London Gazette, 26 Feb. 1878), and on two other occasions; was promoted Major, half-pay, given the Brevet of Lieutenant-Colonel 9 March 1878; received the medal with clasp, and was awarded the Victoria Cross (London Gazette 27 June 1879); "Hans Garrett Moore, Major, 88th Foot. For his gallant conduct in risking his own life in endeavouring to save the life of Private Giese of the Frontier Armed Mounted Police, on the occasion of the action with the Gaikas near Komgha, on the 28th Dec. 1877. It is reported that when a small body of Mounted Police were forced to retire before overwhelming numbers of the enemy, Major Moore observed that Private Giese was unable to mount his horse, and was thereby left at the mercy of the Kaffirs. Perceiving the man's danger, Major Moore rode back alone into the midst of the enemy, and did not desist in his endeavour to save the man until the latter was killed, Major Moore having shot two Kaffirs and received an assegai in the arm during this gallant attempt." A contemporary newspaper says: "the new colonial regiment which is being raised in South Africa for the defence of the Cape Colony will bear the name of its predecessor, the Cape Mounted Rifles, and is to be placed under the command of Brevet Lieut.-Colonel H.Garrett Moore, late of the Connaught Rangers. Capt. R.G. Southey, late of the 2nd Battn. 10th Regt., who recently went out the Cape as a special officer, will act for the present as Second in Command, and Capt. E. G. Brabant, who was for many years connected with the old Cape Regt. And has distinguished himself on several occasions during the late campaign, has been asked to connect himself with the new corps." Brevet Major Moore had been put on half-pay previous to joining the Cape Mounted Police and bought in as a Major into the Argyll and Sutherland Highlanders 15 March 1879. He was – as has been said –given the Brevet of Lieutenant-Colonel, and he became Colonel (Army) 29th April 1882. He resigned the command of the Cape Mounted Rifles in order to serve once more under his old chief, Sir Garnet Wolseley, in the Egyptian Campaign of 1882, as Provost Marshal (A.A. and Q.M.G.) at Headquarters. He was present at the second action at Kassassin and at the Battle of Tel-el-Kebir (Despatches (London Gazette, 2 Nov 1882); Medal with clasp; C.B.; Third Class Osmanieh: Khedive's Star). This was Colonel Moore's last active service, for after commanding his regiment, the 93rd Sutherland Highlanders, now the 2nd Batn. The Argyll and Sutherland Highlanders, he retired, on retired pay as Colonel, having been offered and refused, the rank of Major-General on retired pay. Colonel Moore belonged to a family of great horsemen. His nephew – another Garrett Moore – was the celebrated gentleman rider who won the Grand National in 1879 on his own horse Liberator – a magnificent race. Liberator was third in the Grand National, ridden by Mr Thomas, in 1877. In 1880, he was second to Empress and was ridden by Garrett Moore. He fell in 1881 and 1882. Liberator was quite a character, a cunning old horse, who thought a good deal. He would sort of brush through the fences on the racecourses round London, but he knew he could take no liberties with those at Aintree. Colonel Garrett Moore's family-owned many good horses, amongst others, Rory of the Hills. Colonel Moore, when in India, was Master of the Connaught Rangers' pack of hounds, and he was a good steeplechase rider and the winner of many races. He was also an expert swimmer and yachtsman, and it was owing to his fondness for the last-named pastime that he met his death. On the 5th Oct 1889, Colonel Moore left Portumna Bay in his steam launch, The Foam, accompanied by his stoker, Patrick Byrne, of Banagher. They both went on shore, and Byrne returned to the launch at about half-past nine o'clock. After some time he took in the punt for Colonel Moore, who had dined with General Cooper, and came back with him to the launch at about half-past twelve o'clock. Colonel Moore, however, rowed off in a tremendous gale to secure the rope, which fastened the launch to a buoy. He could not row back against the wind and drifted out into Dromineer Bay. His body was found on Sunday in fourteen feet of water at the Buggaun Island, Urrow Shore. His features were quite unchanged, and he seemed as if he was peacefully asleep. He had never known fear by sight in his life or in his death. He was buried in Mount Jerome Cemetery. The Connaught Rangers have among their regimental plate twenty-five silver goblets, a large number of which were given by officers on St Patrick's Day, 1876. On one of them is inscribed: "Presented by Brevet Major H. G. Moore, 17 March 1876." They have also a silver inkstand, which was presented by Colonel H. G. Moore on leaving the regiment at Cape Town on 7 June 1878. On it is the following inscription: "To the officers of the 88th, The Connaught Rangers. From Brevet Lieut-Colonel H. G. Moore, in Grateful Remembrance of 23 happy Years' Service in the Regiment. Cape Town, 7 June 1878." Colonel Moore was drowned in October 1889, by the capsizing of a boat on a stormy night. Many of the above details are taken from "A History of the Mess Plate of the 88th Connaught Rangers," 1904, by Lieut-Colonel H.F.N. Jourdsin, C.M.G., and most of the rest are supplied by Colonel Moore's niece, Miss Bird. The marquis of Dufferin, when replying, a short time before Colonel Moore's death, to an address of welcome on his return from India, "took occasion to enumerate the names of Irishmen who had distinguished themselves, and mentioned two military men who took precedence of all others – Colonel Moore was one of these."

History of the Victoria Cross, Philip A Wilkins

CHAPTER 7

The Garrett Moores Of Cloghan Castle & The 1640's

The Garrett Moores Of Cloghan Castle & The 1640s

Life was not peaceful in Lusmagh in the 1640s and I am indebted to Mrs Margaret Barton for a copy of the following document, which shows what a shambles the county was in. Bigoe was a French Huguenot who introduced glassmaking in the area. Unfortunately, this entailed the destruction of many trees required for the wood-burning process. It was profitable but unpopular…

Here follows Margaret Barton's copy transcribed from King's County, (Page 87a-89 F.27-1646 T.C.D.)

"Claude Bonny late of Gloaster in the King's County Gent, sworn and examined deposeth and sayeth that he the deponent being by birth a Frenchman came into the kingdom of Ireland about 20 years since, and having until the beginning of the present rebellion lived at Gloaster aforesaid in the faith and religion of a Protestant, he the deponent (amongst many other Protestants his neighbours) was about the 20 of November 1641, and at times since at Gloaster aforesaid and other places forcibly deprived and despoiled of his goods & chattels, & expelled & driven from his habitation & course of living to his now loss & damage of £200 at least, and he is like to be deprived of & loose the future proffettes and benefite of his employment, (worth before the rebellion began £40 annio (per year) and further sayeth that the party that so deprived despoiled & drew him from his habitation were and are these, viz James Kennedie of Ballengarry in Lower Ormond in the County of Tipperary Esq, John Coughlon of Streamstown Esq. Art Molloy of Rathleighan Esq, John OGE McGarrett O'Coughlan of Horne Castle in the King's County Esq, Cosmy Molloy of Cuilly, Gent, Con Coughlan of Milltown, Gent, James O'Coughlan of…… near Gloaster aforesaid, his kinsman Morogh O'Kennedy of Lacken Esq, John OGE Kennedy of Inchrone in the County of Tipperary, Gent, and other complices partakers and followers whoso names he cannot express and further sayeth that at the same time Phillip Bigoe, Gent, Master and owner of the Glasshouse at Gloaster aforesaid was also deprived and robbed of his goods & means at Gloaster aforesaid and other places of very great value, and he the deponent and every other French & English Protestant expelled and driven from thence by the Irish rebells aforesaid _______. From thence (for more saftie) fled to the castle of Newtown alias Ballinoe in the County of Galway, then also belonging to the said Mr Bigoe, where they stood upon their own defence and keeping, for the space of divers moneths, and then they and that castle were besieged by the said James Kennedie, John Coghlan, Art Molloy, John McGarrett O'Coughlan, Cosny Molloy, Con Coghlan, James O'Coghlan, & by Garret Moore of Cloughan in the County of Galway Esq, and the said Morogh O'Kennede, John OGE Kennedi, & by divers others of

the names and septes of the O'Kennedies & O'Hagans of the county of Tipperary in Lower Ormond ______ aforesaid whose chrisson named he knoweth not, and their confederates Phillip Kennedie of or near Loragh in the County of Tipperary Gent, & Art Magoghehan of ______ in the County of Tipperary Gent, Owen OGE O'Madden of Corclegh in the County of Galway Gent, and divers others whose names he cannot express amounting to at least five hundred persons, (which the said rebels continued that siege without ceasing for about 12 days together and the said Phillip Bigoe then & for a long time before, having at his own charge (without relief of any) mentained & kept his said castle of Newtown, 12 soulders, & 42 Protestants men women & children thay defended that castle as well as they could, & with their shott killed many of the rebells & many others they hurt, but the said Bigoe & the deponent & the rest of the soulders being much distressed, especially by want of powder shott ammunition & men, and being also debarred of water and other means of longer subsistence were enforced to submitt so that want, and with much difficulty, gott quarter to come away and depart with their lives, only with 2 muskette 2 swords 2 pirtollstheir apparels and the most part of their other goods, but the said Mr Bigoe was inforced then to give and deliver to those rebells nyntye and furthermore 11 shillings in money to the deponent best remembered, and further sayeth that enen since they fled ot the castle of Newtown aforesaid he & the rest of the household thereof, were so watched & beset & kept soo straightly in the said castle by the rebeld, that the durst not stir publicly abroad, saving that one tyme, Jacob Dehooe, brother in law to the said Mr Bigoe & 4 other soldiers marching privately out of the said castle, were suddenly surprised by an ambush of 300 or 400 rebels, who then & there slew the said Jacob DeHood, but the said other 4 solfiers escaped & fled towards the said castle, and were rescued by such as sallied in their defence out of the same, and afterwards viz about yea month of August 1642 one William Wasbory (who had been one of the soldiers of the said castle) was slain near Balliboy in the King's County, as was going to visit his son whom the rebells has wounded; the wife of the said William Wasbory being but a little before that time hanged by the rebels near Balliboy aforesaid at another time vizt in the year 1642, (to the deponent now best remembrance) one Captain Carroll who then besieged Knocnamoi, and some other rebells, whosso name he knowth not did at the same place near Knocknmoi aforesaid in the King's County hang to death upon a tree, one James Melville a Frenchman whoo was a very zealous Protestant: and the deponent further said that about the month of May 1642, the foresaid Phillip Bigoe and the deponent and some others of their soldiers, privately riding from the said castle of Newtown,mett, by accident with one Donoghoe Deece of Birr in the King's County, Merchant, near unto yea said castle, whom (they suspecting) examined, & searched, & found about him a gun a pistol, a sword, a skeane, and upon searching in his pocket found a letter, written him sent by an from ye rebel Art O'Molloy of Balyleoghan in the King's County Esq, to a Frier in Galway (whoso named the deponent hath now forgotten) whereby he requests that the Frier send him that thing whereof the country stood in most need, & which was the most precious amongst them, and to send

> *to him that what yea price thereof was & had sent monie for it by that, and (upon further search), they found & took from the said Donoghoo tittle £60 in money, & a great leather bagg, wherein had bin gunpowder, which letter the foresaid Mr Bigoe sent afterward to the Lord Clanrickard, and having taken the foresaid Donoghoo into their custody, he the foresaid Donoghoo told them that £20 of the said £60 was the said Art Molloy's own money: wherefore, & for that he the said Mr Bigoe, and the rest conceived (as the deponent yet doth) that the letter was chiefly sent for gunpowder or (being the thing the letter ment & writ for, & desteemed so prescious) he the deponent kept this said £60 and delivered the Donoghoo to yea said Garrett Moore, whoo undertook to bring him before the first Earle of Glifard Howbeith afterwards wheras the said Garrett Moore should deliver him to the said Earle there was a petition put forward to his honour by Nicholas Habbert the sholder of Killian Esq in the name of the said Donoghoo, that this deponent might be command to deliver again to him the said £60, that the said Donoghoo was an honest man and a merchant that only went to buy wares whereupon the deponent received a command from the said Earle either to redeliver the said money or show cause to the contrary, upon which Mr Bigoe had letters from Sir Arthur Blundelnight & Captain Parsons that the foresaid Donoghoo was a notorious rebel, with letters he sent to the said earle, who, (upon view of them) said he would hang him the said Donoghoo O'Deere (as the deponent been told & knoweth as the deponent thinket) and was credible told said Donoghoo was by the said Garreth Moore & Nicholas Habbert or the one of them conveyed away & set at liberty."* - **16th June 1646 Hen Clogher et William Aldrich**

To revert to the life and times of Colonel Garrett Moore M.P. active in the forces of the King in what became known as the Cromwellian Wars from 1641-16; in *Cooke's History of Birr*, we read about the exploits of Colonel Peter Moore (obviously his younger brother) who besieged Birr Castle. There still exists in the archives at Birr Castle, the civilised correspondence of Peter Moore to his neighbour Lady Parsons - who he just happened to be besieging! The following is an excerpt from Cooke's History of Birr, Chapter V:

> *"Sir Laurence Parsons died in the month of September 1628, and was succeeded by his eldest son Richard, a minor, who died in May 1634. Mr William Parsons, second son of Sir Laurence, succeeded his brother; and under the Commission for Remedy of Defective Titles he obtained in 1636, a confirmation of the grant already made to his father. By this new grant he was to hold the premises as a forest at an increased rent.*
>
> *In the commencement of the war of 1641, Mr William Parsons was appointed Governor of Ely O'Carroll and its borders, and also of Birr Castle, which he garrisoned with his tenants to oppose the O'Molloys, O'Carrolls, M'Coghlans, O'Kennedies and Ormonders. From this time forward several skirmishes appear to have taken place between the Birr garrison and the different Irish septs*

surrounding the town; and amongst the rest, an attack was made by the O'Molloy's in December 1641, on the castle of Clonoghill, and an attack was also made by the Irish on the 28th of January following, on the castle of Ballindarra, which was defended by some of the Birr garrison. Both these attacks seem to have been repulsed.

The following circumstances and letters show that the Irish of those days were not the uncultivated people they are sometimes represented to have been, and also prove that there were men of much spirit amongst them. Governer Parsons wrote to Colonel Moore, The Irish commander – whose camp was then at Eglish, a few miles from Birr – to endeavour to bring him over to his side; and promising His Majesty's pardon for the past. The letter, however, was intercepted before reaching its destination by Phelim Molloy, from whose answer, dated 25th of March 1641, the following is an extract;- "Mr Parsons, I intercepted your letter before it came to my Colonel's hands, which, when I perused, I began to be jealous for your partiality, offering your protection to the head and excluding the members from the wings of your mercy. You write to my Colonel forthwith to repair unto you, and to help you in suppressing those who have offended His Majesty; but who are the offenders? The English or the Irish? I say without any partial regard of either nation that they are partly of the Irish, and, for the most part, the English officers and governors, who, contrary to His Majesty's gracious intentions, oppressed the poor subjects, which bred a great scandal to the King's dignity and crown. If you join with them, Mr Parsons, we cannot, in conscience, join in an unlawful matter with you, or with anybody of that fashion, or an fashion else; contrariwise, if you be a true subject, or if God (that I may use your own words) hath yet some share in you, recanting your former life which you have lived these three months last past, I promise you, in my Colonel's name, His Majesty's protection, promising you herby faithfully my best endeavours for the preservation of yourself, your wife, children, and your good mother, whom we held hitherto to be good neighbours, withal assuring you that the good opinion which we conceived of you and your mother was the only case that we behaved ourselves so mild and tender-hearted towards you; which thing your brother-in-law will try by experience to be true, if he be too forward, especially against the poorer sort, whom, as I am informed, he hangs and kills without remorse of conscience, which is no sign of manhood or civil Christianity." *The brother-in-law above referred to was Captain Coote, who was reputed to be very cruel towards the Irish.*

On the 5th of September following, the Lady Parsons' coach-horses were carried away by some of the Irish, and she applied to Colonel Moore to have them restored. His reply – which bears testimony to her popularity, and reflects credit on the soldier who wrote it – was as follows: - 'Much honour's Lady, I received your letter, which might easily move me to do your Ladyship any lawful service, which I have always coveted to do unto all such of your condition, virtue and worth and much the rather for that I find all the gentry and neighbours of these parts to much honour, esteem and love you, and in that degree that one would think you were of their blood and flesh: and they're detained against their will and to their great grief. But, Madam, it pleased God by His will or sufferance that this great alteration and separation of many friends should happen, which hath reduced us to that condition that those who were a little while since loving friends are not burning, killing and destroying one another. And for your part, Madam, though I think you have no malice to us, yet are you the supporter and maintainer of that place, and those that are with you being known, as I hear, to be malicious, will take anything you have to help their designs, as they have used those horses now writ of and by likelihood would do again, so that if I should get them restored, I should arm or help my enemy against myself, in which case (if you were a judge yourself) you would condemn me as much as any. But if I were assured no such use would be made of them, I would endeavour to get them restored, which truly I hold but a poor courtesy and nothing to what I should find myself willing to do for your Ladyship. I would write a little more that might rather tend to your good than otherwise, but that I will not imitate some who stuff their letters with bragging, flaunting and inventing news; but only I wish with all my heart that your Ladyship was out of that danger that some think you are in, for I hear you wish well to all honest people, and so I take leave and remain, your Ladyship's friend and servant in what I may, - P. Moore. Dated the 5th September 1642. To my much honoured and highly esteemed friend, the Lady Anne Parsons, these be presented."

Chapter 8

The Cromwellians

The Cromwellians

It costs a lot of money to raise an army, train it, pay it and equip it. Then you send it into battle.

In ancient Rome when an area was conquered, many of the victorious soldiers were rewarded and paid by grants of land from the defeated territories. It had many advantages. It saved money, kept men of known loyalty in control of the newly acquired lands, and kept the defeated population under close supervision.

The rulers of England and the British Empire had the advantage of a classical education and so knew how to deal with vanquished enemies. The Elizabethans, Cromwellians and Williamites all were rewarded with land grants in Ireland.

I find it very difficult to regard the Scottish Royal Stuart dynasty as anything but a total disaster from King James the First of England, to the 'Young Pretender, Bonnie Prince Charlie' who brought ruin to the Scottish Highlands.

Oliver Cromwell has a very bad name in Ireland, firstly because of his redistribution of most of the good land in the country and his many defeats of the English Royalist and Irish Catholics.

For a different perspective, I would recommend a book called, *Cromwell* by Tom Reilly, a native of Drogheda.

Lt Colonel Axtel was responsible for persuading officers opposing him in Drogheda to surrender to him and, having disarmed them, had them slaughtered. He employed the same tactic at Meelick on the western part of the Cloghan Castle estate. Eighty prisoners were disarmed, tied up and then killed.

Cromwell personally created and trained the most powerful cavalry in Europe at that time. He was a Puritan and he was efficient. Two mortal sins in Ireland. He destroyed a great many fine buildings in Ireland, but not nearly as many as the IRA and the Irish Land Commission after 1922.

The Irish education system has in the past glorified war, which has certainly contributed to our endless strife. In ancient times, the clan chiefs fought so much between themselves that the Normans were able to take over and subdue the whole country.

Chapter 9

1683: Return of the Moores

1683:Return of the Moores

The Moores and Cromwell

There were a number of battles in Lusmagh when the Cromwellian Army arrived. I have a book called, *The Irish Warr of 1641 by a British Officer in the Regiment of Sir John Clottworthy.* It is a description of his battles in Ireland from 1641 to 1653 when the country was laid waste. He wrote:

"In 1650 the Marquis of Ormond left Ireland and made Ulich Bourke, Marquis of Clanrickarde, his deputy. He was true to the King and a good Roman Catholic." We read on page 139: "The Lord Deputy sent his forces under the command of Lieutenant-General Farrell, to a place called Lushmach, where they were encamped a fortnight, expecting more forces daily, and where they expected no enemy without notice. When on a sudden, in an evening, falls on their out-guards a strong party of Horse and Foot of Cromwell's Army, under the command of Sir Jerom (Sankey), and one Colonel Axtel, Governer then of Kilkenny; where after a smart opposition, the Irish having no horse there, were disordered and routed but not above eighty killed; making their escape by boates and Cotts they had near the place and some by swimming over the river. Of the few officers who were killed, one Major Shane O'Hagan was the chiefest, who at the first charge dropt, and who was known to be a good soldier and a stout man.

This Axtell was he that commanded the foot guard that day the good King Charles the first was murdered at his own palace gate, the 30th January, 1648. And after this King's restoration, was executed at Tyburn the year '62, with other Regicides, who at his death said, that he repented nothing more he did in his days, than some unhappy act fell into his hands in Ireland. Which by inquiry we found out afterwards, that he being Governor of Kilkenny, a before said, he killed or caused to kill sixteen or seventeen poor countrymen on protection in that country, and took away their goods, as in those days it was nothing to kill an Irishman, or send them to America for ten pounds apiece, if he had not about him to produce a certificate of taking the Oath of Engagement, as it was so called, which Oath was *in haec verba*: "*I, A.B., do hereby declare that I renounce the pretended title of Charles Stuart and the whole line of late King James, and of every other person pretending to the Government of Nations of England, Scotland and Ireland and Dominions and Territories thereunto belonging; and that I will by the Grace and Assistance of Almighty God, be true and faithful to this Commonwealth, against my King, single person and house of peers, and every of them and hereunto I subscribe my name.*" Who took not this Covenanting Oath was not to have (English or Scottish) the Benefit of the Law, nor the Irish, protection of their lives, as many of them suffered inhumanely."

The population of Ireland was reduced to just over one million and it was said that five-sixths of the people had perished and the countryside left a barren wilderness. (This was certainly an exaggeration.) In 1652, it was possible to travel twenty miles and not see a living creature. Ireland was a country previously noted for the abundance and cheapness of its food. This destruction was followed by the Cromwellian confiscation of land, which effectively changed the ownership of most of Ireland. The Cromwellians blew up Redwood Castle (which was later re-built) and garrisoned Cloghan Castle. They did not damage Cloghan, but turned it into a major fortress for two companies of soldiers. Then came the next Civil War. There were several battles in and around Lusmagh during the years of war between forces loyal to King William and Irish Catholics loyal to James II. We do not know if the castle itself was attacked, although it was taken by a Captain Parsons from Birr Castle in 1691 after the Battle of Aughrim.

However, Mr T L Cooke, author of *The History of Birr*, sheds some light on that time period since Cooke purchased an interesting book in the Cloghan Castle auction of 1852. This book was the *Almanac of Garrett Moore*, which was later shown to the *Royal Society of Antiquaries of Ireland* in 1862.

The Cromwellians took Cloghan Castle in 1651 and remained there until removed by Act of Parliament in 1683. I quote from the Lynch/Moore petition to the House of Lords 1745:

> *"The family being Papists and who were then in possession of the lands concerned in the rebellion in Ireland (which began upon the 23rd October 1641) all their estates were seized and sequestered and controlled in the hands of the usurping powers, till the restoration of his late Majesty King Charles II and by the Act of Settlement made in the 14th and 15th years of his reign, these (amongst other sequestered lands) were declared to be forfeit and absolutely vested the Crown for the purposes of that Act; but Colonel Garrett Moore (who was the heir of the family) having faithfully served his Majesty in his army for many years before his exile and afterwards in his wars abroad and being for that reason an object of his Majesty's favour, prevailed upon his majesty to grant him the estates which formerly belonged to his ancestors; and accordingly, by a particular clause in the Act of Parliament made in the 17th and 18th year of King Charles II for explanation of the before mentioned Act of Settlement it was enacted that The Commissioners for the execution of that Act should restore to him, his heirs and assigns all the manors and estates, which he or his father held or enjoyed or ought to have held, possessed or enjoyed up to 22nd October 1641."*

And the commissioners were to allot to the adventurers and soldiers and their heirs, who should be removed to make way for such restitution, a satisfaction out of other undisputed forfeit lands.

That Act effectively tells us who took over Cloghan Castle during the Cromwellian Era, so back came Garrett now only 83 years old. His Almanac last heard of in Mayo some fifty years ago surfaced in 1852 and parts of it were copied and I give some of it as follows.

The title of the MS is *Garett Moore, his Almanack & pocket book, without beginning & without end 1699.* It contains rules for using a new perpetual 'card' or almanac, and similar matters; also quack recipes, and obscene ribaldry. At page 32 is drawn a quadrant, and between 32-33 are inserted 'cards' to which the rules refer; they are circular, drawn on two pieces of strong vellum, 4 inches in diameter. One is signed 'Solomon Grisdall', the other 'Garett Moore, An. 1699'. At p. 34-35, are field notes of a survey and a map of Oxmantown Green, Dublin. At page 30 occurs the following quatrain: "If any now offended by, with him, I say, yet pend it; let him, I pray, without delay, go take his pen & mend it."

"Garrett Moore Philomath & Almanack Maker lately come from Germany "after a very tedious study". But the greatest novelty, and certainly one which, if true, would be invaluable to an assassin, is the entry on page 37, of which the following is a copy:

> *"A secret to make bullets that will scatter like shott. –First, take one ounce of lead, and soe much of salamoniack as you can take between two fingers, and one ounce of Quick-Silver, melt all together and make bullets – one bullet will doe execution in nature of shott; How to make powder that will make no report.-Take a charge of powder and putt it in a pair of scales, and mix it with the like quantity of burned alum, then charge ye gun or pistol."*

It is all a bit eccentric to say the least, but some of it is written when he was 100 years old, so I think we should not be too critical! When the self same Colonel Garrett Moore wrote his will five years later it commenced: *"In the name of God, Amen. I Garrett Moore of Moate in the County of Mayo, Esq., being of good health and sound memory (God be everlastingly praised) do make my last will and testament hearing I have to die and that the time of dissolution is near".* – etc, etc.

The Williamite Wars were over, Cloghan Castle was in the possession of the Protestant forces but he had been clever enough to previously place most of his property in trust with his Protestant friends. His Almanac may have been eccentric, but he was no fool. He did not intend that the Moore family would have their lands confiscated again, but alas, even more was to follow – The famous lawsuit!

Extract from Almanac continues:

> *"Wee Edward Croe of Tullynedaly in the County Galway, Esq., and Jasper Ousley of Doonmore in ye said County Gent. Doe by these p'sents for vs our Extors adtrs and assignes Demise Release and for ever Quit Claime unto Garett Moore of Cloonbigny in the County of Roscomon Gent. And Bridgett Bodkin alias Moore of Cloonbigny afore said their heires Extors and administrators all and all manner of actions, cause and causes of actions, Challenges and demandes which wee or either of us have to or against the said Bridgett Bodkin alias Moore and the said Garett Moore or either*

of them on the acc.ts of Carronroe or any other acc.ts whatsoever from the beginning of the World to the aforesaid day of May 1702. In witness where of wee have hereunto sett our hands and seales this sixteenth day of October 1704.

Being p'sent,

"Edward Brown,	*Ed: Crow.*
Daniell Surridge,	*Jasper Ousley"*

There was also, at p. 87, an agreement to abide by an award or arbitrators in a case of dispute about tithes between Captain Roger O'Shaugnessy and Mrs Allice Moore, dated April 10th, 1700; witnessed, inter alios, by "Ga: Moore". At p. 88, the following curious entry, bearing on the value of stock and money, occurred:

"June 14, 1703. Bought then of Dermott Carrony two dry Cowes for one pound eleven shillings, one of them being a branded Cow and one brown heffer, the same day bought from him one black melsh Cow with a Cow Calfe for one pound, he is to find graseing for the said melsh Cow until May next in consideration of the milke which he is to have. He is obliged to give me six shill for the Calfe next May if it be my choise or if any thing happens the said Calfe, he is to find graseing for the dry Cowes until Micaelmus next.

The particulars of the mony paid him:

One gin att,	*1 03 0*
2 plate cobes att,	*0 09 6*
2 Milled Crownes att,	*0 10 10*
1 perru Cob att,	*0 04 06*
1 ½ plate att,	*0 02 04 ½*
1 Scotch shill att,	*0 00 10*
One ½ penny att,	*0 00 00 ½*
	£2 11 1
The sum….	*2 11 0*
Over paid,	*00 00 1*

The items relative to the Castle of Cloghan at p. 130 were as follows:

"Led for the Castle of Cloghan. The Norwest flanker 6 foot long and 3 foot breadth. South West flanker 3 foot long and 3 foot breadth.

Nor est & South Est each flanker is 6 foot long and 3 in breadth.

4 pipes for the 4 flankes, each pipe 2 ½ foot long and 13 inches in breadth.

A sheet of 5 foot long and 3 foot in breadth will make ye pipes."

At p. 46, was the following meteorological entry:

"On the 20th of May 1704 fell a shower of Blood in the Est side of the Suberbs of the town of Loughrea in ye County of Galway which was visible on the stones and dockes for a good while after."

It may also be of interest to some persons to give the headings of "*The Use and Explanations*" of the circular card almanac inserted in the book:

1st To finde ye key day and leape yeare forever

2nd To finde ye Epact forever.

3rd To know ye number of each month & ye day of ye month forever.

4th To know ye Age of ye Moon for ever.

5th To find Easter forever, and consequently all ye movable feasts.

6th To find ye beginning & end of ye Law Terms forever.

7th To find ye Imoveable feasts & other Emenent dayes forever.

8th To find the Suns rising & setting with ye length of ye day and night forever.

9th To find ye Suns place in the Eccliptick any day forever.

10th To find ye time of ye moones southing any day forever.

11th To find how long ye moon shines any night or morning forever.

12th To find ye time of heigh water forever at certain places named (63 in number, in England, Scotland, Ireland and on the Continent)

13th To find ye moons riseing and setting any time of her shining forever."

There are also, at pp. 22-30, rules:

"To find ye Golden number. To find ye dominical letters forever. To know when it is Leap year forever. To find ye Roman Indiction forever."

Banagher was occupied by the Irish Royalist Catholic side in the war between King William and King James II, whilst Birr was in the hands of the Williamite Protestant forces. Cloghan Castle was held by the Jacobite Royalist forces of Colonel Oxburgh's regiment. We have found "Gun Money" dated 1689 on the front park where the Irish Jacobite Army was camped. Also found was an old razor and many buckles from horses' harnesses. When the Catholic army was defeated in the nearby Battle of Aughrim in 1691, the Jacobites left Banagher and a Protestant force was sent by Captain Parsons of Birr to take Cloghan Castle in which he then left a Garrison of soldiers under command of Lt. Archibald Armstrong.

Between July 1690 and the Battle of Aughrim in 1691, there were a whole series of small battles and skirmishes between the Irish Jacobite forces in Banagher, Cloghan Castle and two other Castles and the Williamite forces in Birr. In effect, the whole area was a battleground with the Jacobites mostly the winners. In the North, the Jacobites held Athlone and defended it successfully against the Williamites, whilst the Williamites, against attacking Jacobites, successfully defended Birr Castle.

In 1688, Garrett Moore was a member of the Jacobite Corporation of Banagher. In a list of Kings County Jacobites pardoned under the Limerick and Galway Articles (of surrender) appears the name of Col. Garrett Moore. He was allowed to stay in Ireland and return his estates for taking an Oath of Allegiance to William & Mary. I doubt if he was our Garrett who was well over 80 years old at the time!

The famous lawsuit between the Lynch-Blosses and the Moores lasted over 100 years and effectively ruined the losing side – the final loser being Garrett O'Moore who was bankrupted in 1852. This lawsuit was based on Genealogy and inheritance, and in my opinion, it is the only logical reason for the Garrett Moore who inherited in the early eighteen hundreds to suddenly become an Irish Clan Chief! Garrett was a lawyer and he commanded the Clanrickarde Chasseurs, which was a yeomanry regiment rather akin to the Territorial (part-time) Army in Britain today. An earlier Garrett had married Lady Mary Burke, daughter of the 9th Earl of Clanrickarde. This gentleman got Sir John Betham to produce a pedigree showing that far from being a Barmeath Moore, he was now a descendant of Rory O'More and thus "The O'Moore". It sounded great but fooled nobody except his own family and it certainly did not for one moment fool the Lynch-Blosses in their many lawsuits. Colonel 'The O'Moore' of Cloghan Castle in the King's County sounded great but it was nonsense. His real pedigree was every bit as noble as the one he claimed.

Ireland is full of amateur Genealogists who like to spot a fake. In recent times, we have had a fake Baron (known as the 'Bogus Baron') and a claimant to a very ancient clan chieftainship who made a lot of friends by handing out his own medals and awards before being exposed by someone whose own antecedents were possibly as bogus!

A Colonel O'Moore of Cloghan Castle appears in Croker's, *Life of Oliver Goldsmith.* If this is so, then it places him in that magic circle surrounding the great Doctor Johnson, which included Burke, Goldsmith and Joshua Reynolds. In the *Life of Goldsmith*, the following story appears:

> *"So remarkable a feature of his (Goldsmith's) character was this extreme unwillingness that any other should, for whatever cause, share that attention which he thought exclusively due to himself, that his companions sometimes took advantage of it to make him appear in a very ridiculous light. The following story, which, if related of any other man, would scarcely obtain credit, on any evidence, is told by Mr Croker, on the authority of his friend, Colonel O'Moore, who was himself present on the occasion: - 'One afternoon, as Colonel O'Moore and Mr Burke were going to dine with Sir Joshua Reynolds, they observed Goldsmith, also on his way to Sir Joshua's, standing near a crowd of people, who were staring and shouting at some foreign women in the windows of one of the houses in Leicester Square. "Observe Goldsmith", said Mr Burke to O'Moore, "and mark what passes between him and me by and by at Sir Joshua's". They passed on, and arrived before Goldsmith, who came soon after, and Mr Burke affected to receive him very coolly. This seemed to vex poor Goldsmith, who begged Mr Burke would tell him how he had had the misfortune to offend him. Burke appeared very reluctant to speak, but, after a good deal of pressing, said, 'that he was really ashamed to keep up an intimacy with one who could be guilty of such monstrous indiscretions as Goldsmith had just exhibited in the Square.' Goldsmith with great earnestness protested he was unconscious of what was meant. 'Why', said Burke, 'did you not exclaim, as you were looking up at those women, what stupid beasts the crowd must be for staring with such admiration at those painted Jezebels, while a man of your talents passed by unnoticed?' Goldsmith was horror-struck, and said, 'Surely, surely, my dear friend, I did not say so?' – 'Nay', replied Burke, 'if you had not said so, how should I have known it?'-'That's true', answered Goldsmith, with great humility; 'I am very sorry – it was very foolish' I do recollect that something of that kind passed through my mind, but I did not think I had uttered it.'"*

Some years ago, when my wife and I were going through the Frick Museum in New York, we saw two small portraits on loan to the museum of a Mr and Mrs Moore by Sir Joshua Reynolds. I am pretty certain that these were the Moores from Cloghan Castle, but I have been unable to trace them again.

Chapter 10

1689 – 1690
The Jacobites

1689 - 1690 The Jacobites

1683

This was the year that King Charles II discovered a strong Protestant plot to overthrow him. The plotters were killed without mercy and the King had to gain more friends. It was then, I think, that he suddenly recalled all those loyal Catholic supporters who had lost their lands and petitioned for them to be returned. Having ignored them for years, he remembered them and I think, but do not know, that Colonel Garrett Moore was one of the happy recipients of the King's belated gratitude.

Colonel Oxburgh's Regiment 1689 – 1690

Not Good Years for Ireland

Colonel Garrett Moore may have been eccentric, but he was no fool. 1683 was the year the Moore properties were returned to him and he promptly put them in a family Trust. The Trustees were all good Protestants.

When King Charles II died, his younger brother James became King and, as he was a Catholic, began to bring Catholicism to the English. This was unpopular, and he was replaced on the throne by his daughter Anne and her husband the Protestant Dutch Prince William of Orange. James promptly fled to Ireland to gather supporters. He arrived in Kinsale, county Cork, and was met by the Governors of Kinsale, and my Catholic 8th great-grandfather, Colonel The O'Donovan, who had his own regiment of 1,200 men.

James headed north gathering soldiers as he went and eventually reached the walled city of Londonderry where a Protestant ancestor of mine, Alderman Henry Thompson, was waiting. A band of young Apprentices closed the city gates to the oncoming King and a siege began. It lasted 105 days. The city lay in ruin and some 10,000 innocent Protestants died. On 6th June 1689, a bomb killed Alderman Thompson and destroyed his home.

A substantial force previously sent by King William to relieve the Siege, had sat, waiting, only a few miles away.

Whilst all this was going on in Northern Ireland, the Jacobite army of King James II, in the guise of Colonel Oxburgh and his Company, occupied Cloghan Castle. From Cloghan Castle, they attacked Birr Castle. The soldiers were paid "Gun Money" i.e. coins made from melted cannon with a picture of James II and dated the month and year. If the Jacobites won, they would be well off. If they lost, then the coins were worthless. Many years later, we used to find some of the coins in the emplacements and also in our avenue of ancient yew trees.

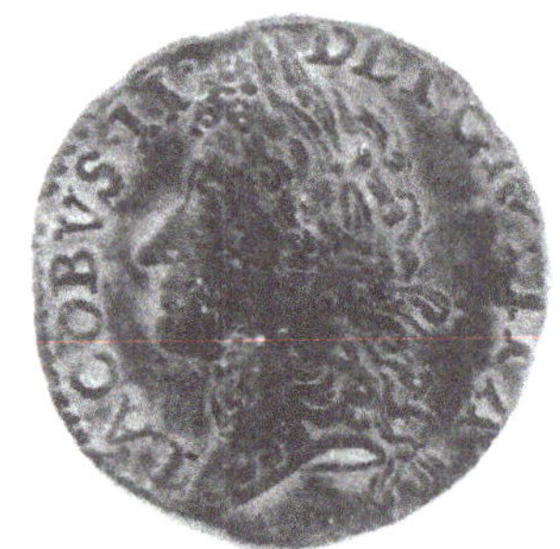

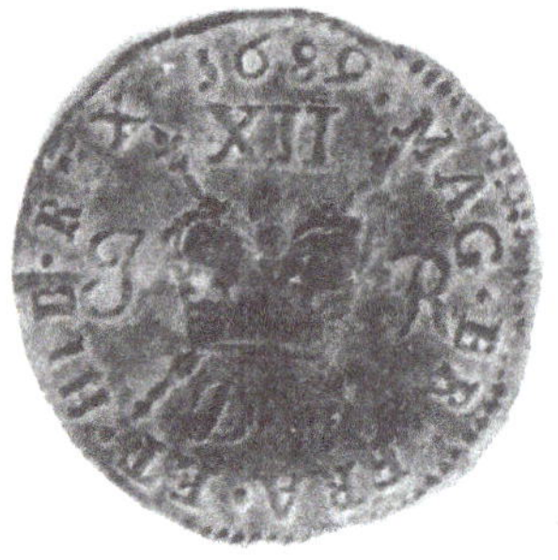

Gun Money found in Cloghan Castle

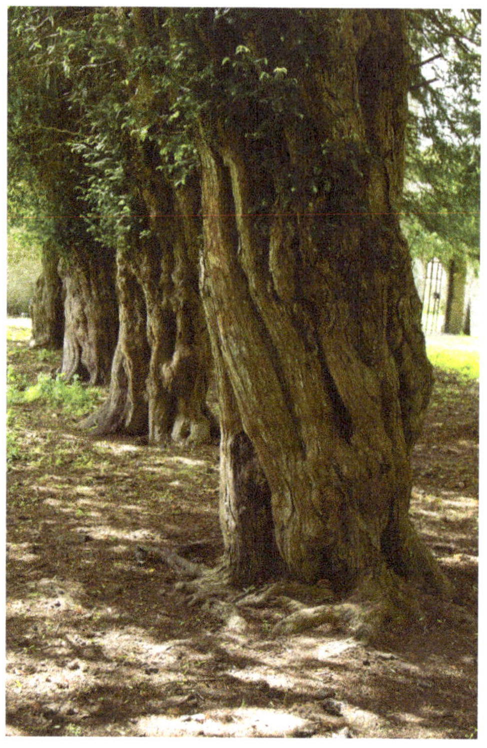

Ancient Yew trees on the grounds of Cloghan Castle

The siege of Derry was ended by a brave sailor who broke the boom across the River Foyle. The Jacobites moved South. The comfortably situated and well-fed General of the Williamite army marched for a couple of hours to the city, where he promptly disbanded and disarmed the Citizen army – who had been the main defenders – and then dismissed them without pay.

The Battle of the Boyne led to the defeat of the Jacobites, which was followed by the Battle of Aughrim. Colonel Oxburgh and his men left Cloghan Castle to be replaced by an ancestor of Lord Rosse from Birr Castle.

Colonel Garrett Moore got the castle back, because it was owned by a 'Protestant Trust' and he himself was an old man not involved in any battles.

Colonel the O'Donovan was defeated in battle by Colonel Churchill (later the Duke of Marlborough) and he and his sons were declared outlaws.

William Thompson, son of Alderman Henry, petitioned the King for compensation for loss during the siege. William was not paid a penny and then, in 1704, was made a second class citizen (i.e. Protestant non-conformist) and removed from the walled city as were all the other Thompsons. For 150 years, they lived in the land…OUTSIDE the city walls.

The Jacobite army retreated – into Limerick city for a long siege. When finally defeated, some soldiers went home, some went to serve the Kings of France and Spain, and others joined the English army, so that, for instance, the Devonshire Regiment became largely manned by Irish ex-Jacobites.

This copied the event at the end of the Cromwellian war, when some of the defeated Irish were imprisoned in the Aran Islands, some ran home, some were sent as slaves to the West Indies, and the rest joined the Cromwellian Army!

Chapter 11

The 1798 Revolution and Local Battles

The 1798 Revolution and Local Battles

The revolutions in America and France inspired a wave of new ideas in many countries. In Ireland, Presbyterians and Catholics joined together to form the 'United Irishmen' and with the help of France, a rebellion was planned.

Unfortunately, the plot was discovered and the rising was put down amidst great ferocity on both sides.

When the British left Ireland in 1922, they left behind their records in Dublin Castle. One can imagine how interested our local historians were when, just a few years ago, they discovered letters from a secret government informer writing to his master in Dublin Castle in 1798 about the people of Lusmagh.

They learnt that Garrett Moore of Cloghan Castle was thought to be sympathetic to the rebels, i.e. a United Irishman. The name of the government spy, whose descendants still live here, has not been disclosed. For their part in the rebellion, three Lusmagh men were hanged on their own front doors, and a member of the Larkin family was flogged, by the Military in Banagher. I have included an extract below, describing an incident involving both Redwood and Cloghan Castles, which, comes straight from the Reverend John Gleeson's book, *History of Ely O'Carroll,* first published in 1915.

"James Meany, Outlaw"

"We have now travelled over a space of twelve hundred years; the monks are all gone, the O'Kennedy's have just left Lackeen, the MacEgan is reduced to comparative poverty, living on two hundred and fifty acres of land; the old castle of Redwood-Coillte Ruadh is a ruin; the rebellion of 1798 has been suppressed, and thus we come to the last incident in the story of Redwood Castle. The ruined Castle has now become the refuge of an outlaw and his companions. The name of the outlaw is James Meany. The narrative of Meany's life and adventures has come down to us in a manuscript, whose author is not known, as the flyleaf of the manuscript has disappeared. It runs as follows:

James Meaney, commonly called the Bold Captain, was a celebrated character in the southwest of Ireland at the close of the eighteenth century. His name is well remembered by the peasantry of the surrounding district in which he chiefly figured. He was born in the year 1770 at Teneseragh in the Co. Galway. His father had been a respectable farmer; but, having had a large family, James removed to a place called Kilnacross, near Redwood, in the Co. Tipperary. There he rented about thirty acres of land. In this place he lived quietly for some years; his principal feats having been performed at the hurling, so common about that period. At these gatherings, he distinguished himself so much that he acquired a considerable share of popularity, ultimately to his ruin.

Meany, who was fairly educated, possessed a rare intelligence very much superior to that of his companions. Sensitive and of an ardent temperament, he keenly felt the many wrongs under which his country laboured at that time. In consequence, he enlisted under the banners of the United Irishmen, when their organisation spread. For many reasons, he was soon selected as one of their captains in his district. Of almost gigantic stature, combined with great physical strength, wonderful agility and swiftness of foot, Meany was immediately welcomed as a most desirable acquisition by that society. His zeal and earnestness were appreciated; and he was taken a good deal into the confidence of the Directory. Under his local leadership, a large number hailed him as their captain.

But after the premature outbreak of '98, poor Meany was at once marked to surrender; but suspecting the punishment, which awaited, if he obeyed the order, he refused to comply with the request. Then he was outlawed, and orders given that he should be taken either dead or alive. Meany was thus driven to extremity, and determined to fight to the last, he took refuge in the picturesque old castle of Redwood. Being well acquainted with the people of the neighbourhood, he was loved by them for his courage and misfortunes, and received from them assistance so far as it could be privately rendered. The small chamber or cell in Redwood Castle, where Meany lay concealed for so long a time, was approached by a perilous flagway or gallery. The dimly lighted cell is called after his name to the present day.

There he was surrounded and secretly fed by his followers. Whenever danger loomed in the distance, he had timely notice through watchful and intelligent friends. Some outlaws, like himself, shared the fortunes of their forlorn captain; and under his leadership they gathered blackmail from the surrounding gentry, who had been most distinguished for their violent behaviour during the rebellion. Elevated from the earth, in his romantic eyrie, Meany called a council of war one stormy night towards the close of 1799. It was then proposed by a member of the company (as they could exist no longer without having recourse to extreme means) that for the purpose of securing supplies, they should attack the mansion of a gentleman named O'Carroll. This popular gentleman's house was seven miles away at a place called Kilfadda.

'Now,' said the rascal who made the proposal, 'begorra I'm courtin' the cook myself, and I can give the craythur a whisper not to bar the door, for she is mortal fond of me; and resave the haporth we'll have to do in this wide, earthly world but rise the latch. Then the matter is done, boys, in a jiffy, and keep our powder dry for the yeomen. Now ye see there will be no trouble at all, at all'

To this dishonourable proposal Meany stoutle demurred for some time, because he particularly shrunk from attacking the old gentleman, who was beloved in the neighbourhood. Moreover, in O'Carroll's younger days he had been one of the most deadly shots, and an expert swordsman. He was regarded as a celebrated duellist in the province to which he belonged, and the terror he inspired caused many of the Cromwellians in Tipperary to lower their pretensions. The outlaw's remonstrance's were over-ruled by the majority of his band; and he was obliged to yield an unwilling assent to their project.

Accordingly, the night was fixed, and Kilfadda Castle fell an easy prey to the raiders. Meany did all he could to save whatever property was exposed, and to prevent personal injury being done to the inmates. But the country people never forgave the outrage. O'Carroll was one of the old stock, and almost regarded as a chieftain by his friends. Meany was now obliged to quit his safe retreat in Redwood Castle, because he feared that if information were given to the military, he would be surrounded. Consequently he sought refuge in Lusmagh Parish in the King's County.

On one occasion, when returning alone from a neighbour's house to this lair, Meany encountered a body of yeomen, known as Colohan's Corps. Espying them from a distance, and coming towards him, his resolution was at once taken. For he knew Colohan's Corps to be the most bloodthirsty of all the dogs of war let loose on the country; they were also the greatest cowards that ever disgraced uniform. Trusting in good luck, Meany lay down behind a hedge bordering the road near a small plantation; on the yeomen coming near he stood boldly up and ordered pretended companions in the wood to be quiet but ready. He then deliberately fired at Colohan, who was in front.

The gallant captain immediately turned his horse and fled, followed by his company. Meany still shouted, and fired shots in quick succession, for he was well armed, until the yeomen had disappeared. However, this encounter proved unfavourable to him; it was now known that he was hiding in the neighbourhood, and a large body of troops was ordered from Banagher to scour the neighbourhood.

Meany was concealed in a cave surrounded by woods, and situated not far from Cloghan Castle, at that time the seat of the well-known Colonel Moore, so often mentioned in the life of our national poet, Goldsmith. Here he might have lain concealed for many a day, if he had not been betrayed either through fear or jealousy, people say the latter, of a girl who brought him food from a farmer's house. Whatever her motive was, it is certain that this damsel gave information to the authorities. The soldiers came direct to the place she pointed out; and, on Meany appearing, to learn what was the matter; a dozen muskets were levelled; immediately as many bullets passed through his body. His mangled remains were carried into town, and there hung up in chains in the market-place, according to the custom of that time.'

How many other unrecorded episodes, connected with this fine Castle, have been forgotten? They must be left to the imagination of writers of romance. How easily might an Irish writer of ability emulate Walter Scott in weaving Irish romance into the story of our ruins, and of ancient families, who held high rank in the centuries, which we have been considering! Irish literature would then rise to a higher level, and would help to revive the self-respect and national spirit of the people."

What a long way we've come since 1915.

Travelling back to this era, we come across the following which I also give to you verbatim from a parish paper and from a book entitled *The Irish Faction Fighters of the 19th Century*:

"Faction Fights"

"The faction fighting of 19th century Ireland was a strange social phenomenon, which had its origin just South of us in Co. Tipperary. It spread like wildfire and soon factions were fighting each other in many counties.

Factions were armies of country people, armed usually with sticks and stones and sometimes even with swords and guns. Their fights were between families, clans, baronies or parishes. The remote cause of the fighting was some insult, real or imaginary. They usually fought for the sheer love of fighting and the battlefields were gair greens, market places and the streets of towns and villages. Many people were killed and scores wounded in the more notorious and awesome fights.

"T'would bate Banagher and Banagher bate the Devil" was an old saying commonly heard in Ireland to express amazement at a very unusual occurrence. It could have been related to a tragic faction fight in the town of Banagher on 6th January 1814 when 500 fighters from the parish of Lusmagh marched in "with the intention of beating Banagher." A two-day advance notice of their intention was posted prominently in the twon. The notice from "Captain Stout" read something like this. "We the parishioners of Lusmagh give notice to the town of Banagher that we will go in on Thursday next and give them battle. Every man jack from 12 to 60 will turn out. We defy the best yeomen of Captain Armstrong. We will disarm them and take the town. Let ye rue the hour that we go in."

The men of Lusmagh had for many years, at fairs and markets on church holidays, been vying with those of Banagher to decide which was the better at the popular sport of stick fighting. Fights had taken place between the champions of the Parish and the town. But this was different. Lusmagh was now intent on forcing full-scale battle on Banagher. The earlier sporting rivalry had given place to bitter enmity. The enmity was of longer duration, as we shall see. Lusmagh and Banagher were in the Barony of Garrycastle. Lusmagh is also an ancient territory in its own right under the jurisdiction of the O'Hoolaghans and the O'Maddens.

The territory around Banagher had been the possession of the MacCoughlans for 500 years. In 1539 one Felim MacCoughlan was slain by the sons of Malachy O'Madden after Sunday mass at Banagher. The families were "in contention" from that point in time and so the rivalry between Lusmagh and Banagher was already centuries old in 1814. Furthermore, the English Garrison of Banagher was often attacked by the men of Lusmagh. So faction fights in other places owes much less to tradition than did this fight at Banagher. The people were talking about it and preparing for it since the harvest of 1813. One Brian Carroll was so skilled with his fighting stick that "he could 'croost' a robineen going through a skylight".

At the time of the 1814 faction fight, Banagher had 2,650 inhabitants and Lusmagh had 3,400 parishioners.

The magistrate Captain Lt. George Armstrong (who lived at Mountcharles, Banagher) was known as a liberal forthright man who would take no nonsense from anyone. There was a rumour going around that he would take sides in the coming fight with a view to teaching the Lusmaghites a lesson that they would never forget. Apparently, he intended to call out the local yeomen, give them their head on the side of Banagher. At the same time as magistrate, he would apply for regular military and use them to stop the fight.

Despite the condemnation by their Parish Priest, the men of Lusmagh began to gather early on the morning of 6th January 1814. They marched in fours along the narrow side-roads and converged on the main Birr-Banagher road. Witnesses said there must have been nearly a thousand of them, armed mainly with blackthorns, oak sticks and bags of stones. A few who carried swords, scythes, knives and blunderbusses did not intend to use them unless the townsmen first brought similar weapons into the fight. It was to be a fair fight with sticks and stones.

The town of Banagher was early astir to repel the invaders. Shop-windows remained shuttered. Barricades of carts and furniture were built in the main street. Arrangements were made ready for the treatment of casualties.

When the Lusmagh men got into the outskirts of Banagher they formed into lines across the street, but there wasn't a townsperson to be seen. On entering the main street, however, they found themselves faced by the Banagher men who had also drawn up lines. It was just after 9 o'clock. The Lusmagh men halted, all their forces not having come up yet. According to the general plan of action, some groups had already entered the side streets. Meeting with no opposition, these groups soon converged on the main street and swelled the great crowd, which was assembled there.

While waiting for the action to commence, the main body of the Lusmagh men wheeled and hurled other insults at the townspeople. Stones were exchanged, but there was no close-quarter action until the Lusmagh leaders, Brian Carroll and Joseph Larkin, placed themselves at the head of their men. The attack must begin at once, they said, and matching their words with action, started forward, their sticks at the ready. Three Banagher men advanced against them, brandishing their sticks. Shouting "Lusmagh Abu" Carroll and Larkin drove the three men back in a flurry of sticks.

Another party of Lusmagh men entered the main street, beating a number of Banagher citizens before them, and linked up with their own main body which then surged forward. The men of Banagher advanced to meet them, both sides shouting their faction cries, and they met with a great cracking of sticks. Lines wavered and buckled. Witnesses said that yeomen not in uniform were fighting on the Banagher side.

A new element entered the fight as, above the noise and the clamour, military orders were shouted and men in the bright red and blue uniforms of the 12th Regiment thrust their way through the Banagher men. The soldiers then straddled the street between the rival factions and, although assailed by showers of Lusmagh stones, they held their ground and their fire. They were charged by parties of the Lusmagh men, some of whom broke through and resumed fighting the Banagher men behind the military lines.

Captain Armstrong was trying to stop the fighting. But it continued regardless of him and of the soldiers, who were pushed and beaten until they managed to extricate themselves from a difficult position. Larkin was reported to be jumping up and down like a maniac, urging on the Lusmagh men. Although he was a small man, he had a reputation for ferocity and was said to be very deft with his stick. He went down the street in an attempt to get more of his men into the fight. Many of them, not over-enthusiastic about confronting the troops, were hanging back. Some began to attack a house in which about a score of Banagher men had taken refuge.

What followed is not quite clear but Captain Armstrong did cause a detachment of the 12th regiment to be marched to the scene of the fight and a coroner's jury was to find that he ordered fire to be opened on the Lusmagh men. This the military did, killing three and wounding twelve. Fighting was ended when the soldiers opened fire. The townspeople immediately joined the Lusmagh men in doing what they could for the casualties after which the men from the parish retired sorrowfully to their homes."

Chapter 12

Visitors And the 1840s Famine

Visitors And the 1840s Famine

We once had a visit from a Mr Thomas Clayton of New York whose great grandfather wrote a book called, *Scenes and Incidents in Irish Life* which depicted incidents in the life of his father in the period 1800-1805. I am very grateful to Mr T E Clayton who in 1982 sent me an excerpt from the book written by his grandfather Francis Harry Clayton using the name of Claymore referring to his grandfather in 1800-1805:

> *"Within about three miles of Banagher, on the banks of the River Brosna, stood a grand old castle called Cloghan Castle, the residence of a Major O'Moore, a fine specimen of an Irish gentleman, somewhat like the late Mr. D'Arcy, only more blunt and more blustering. He kept open house and entertained to excess, was never without visitors, a person of about fifty, portly and fond of hunting, always possessing a number of splendid horses for saddle or harness, a keen sportsman, whether in the hunting field or with dog and gun. His wife was a most amiable and agreeable person about ten years the Major's junior. They had a family of two sons, aged eighteen and twenty years respectively; many a day and night did Claymore spend at Cloghan Castle, together with some brother officers.*
>
> *A long avenue of a mile between the first and second gate led to the castle; great beech, chestnut and oak trees lined the avenue and dotted the demesne with its tufts of daffodils and other flowers scattered here and there. After passing through the second gate and sweeping round a curve you came in front of the castle, whose turreted walls towered above, and seemed to nestle amongst the grand old trees thickly surrounding it. The lawn in front was profusely covered with flowers, the whole scene and surroundings were that of sequestered peacefulness, too much so for the Major and his wife, but that was remedied by the unceasing flow of visitors, and oft recurring dinner and other parties, at almost all of which Claymore was present."*

Famine

By the 1840s, the railways and steam-driven ships on the Shannon had transformed travel in the locality. However, a huge population explosion, the landlord/tenant system and the potato were factors that were about to destroy the old fabric of Irish life forever.

When the potato blight struck year after year, it caused the most terrible hardship, but the calamitous winter of 1847 was the final straw. The Moores had not received rents for years and although they now owned 9,261 acres in four counties. However, their help for their starving tenants, and the Lynch/Moore lawsuits, finally ruined them. The Cloghan Castle estate was sold in bankruptcy in 1852.

In 1840 there were 700 families living in Lusmagh. By 1850, five hundred of those families were gone through starvation, typhus and evictions.

My own great grandmother remembered the famine in County Antrim, and I am quite certain that family memories are equally vivid in Lusmagh, but this is not a matter for discussion as the memory of humiliation and suffering is too vivid in the sub-conscious of the Irish to allow the matter to be fully aired. The people died, the Irish language died, and the population halved from its 9 million!

Dr More Madden, whose memorial can be seen in Meelick Abbey, wrote a book in the 19th century entitled, *The O'Maddens of Hy Many.* I am fortunate to have his own personal notes about his ancestors, his father and his own achievements. This copy has been handed down from one owner of Cloghan Castle to the next, leaving out only one owner who was thought to be unworthy of that trust.

Dr More Madden's father, a Dr Richard Madden FRCS, was a physician with an extensive practice in Mayfair, London until he was appointed by Lord Palmerston to be the British representative in Havana, Cuba for the international commission working on the abolition of the slave trade. In 1840, he was appointed Commissioner of Inquiry on the West Coast of Africa, again in relation to the slave trade and also the state of English settlements. In 1847, he became Colonial Secretary of Western Australia. Dr Madden (Richard) was a prolific writer and published more than 40 books. He was the great-grandson of Daniel Madden, Clan Chief in 1687. Dr Madden wrote the following article:

> *"During one of my visits to Galway, immediately before my departure for the west coast of Africa whither I was despatched by Her Majesty's Special Commissioner in 1841, an incident occurred which made a lasting impression on my mind. I was one day at the Abbey of Meelick, on the banks of the Shannon, near Eyrecourt, Co. Galway, which in the year 1474 was founded by Eoghan O'Madden, Chief of Silanchia, and whilst occupied there taking notes of inscriptions on the tombstones of my ancestors, I was startled by the distant strains of the Caoine or death dirge. Nearer and nearer came that mournful wailing along Shannon's banks, and soon a multitude of people accompanying a funeral entered the Abbey graveyard. From distant districts of the surrounding country they had assembled, and when the internment was over several scattered groups lingered awhile among the ruins of Meelick.*
>
> *At a tomb, near where I stood, knelt some aged men, who in the Gaelic language uttered a requiem over the dead, of my own name and race, the founders of Meelick Abbey. I then spoke to those peasants, whom I found to be remarkably intelligent, and who no sooner learned that I was a stranger in the locality than they hastened to give me every information in their power on the subject of my inquiries. Whilst I was thus listening, one of the Franciscan Fathers of the adjoining convent whom*

I had before known, approached, and warmly renewed acquaintance. After our first greeting was over, he announced my name to the little group who still lingered about, in terms too flattering to be repeated here. Suffice to say that there could scarce have been a scene of greater enthusiasm than was manifested by those warm-hearted people who gathered around me with 'Cead Mile Failte', *hand grasping and good wishes for long life and prosperity – for a scion of the race of the Siol Anmchadha. Nor could I but feel grateful at this demonstration of affection towards the memory of the old line that had passed away.*

I was then conducted by the good Father into the adjoining convent occupied by himself and two other friars – last survivors of the once famous Franciscan community of Meelick, where I received every possible kindness and hospitality during my brief stay in the most interesting locality.

At that time, there was little left of the ancient Abbey but the roofless walls, ruined aisled and beautiful pillars, mouldering into dust to attest its former splendour. Nevertheless, at the time of my visit in 1841, there still existed under the ruined walls of Meelick, the humble friary of the successors of its exiled and murdered monks.

There, so far back as the year 1642, the Sons of St Francis had reassembled from their hiding places in the caves of the hillsides, or in the recesses of the forests on the Shannon's banks. And there, with a brief interval during the Cromwellian reign of terror, they had continued their sacred mission as undeterred by the poverty and obscurity that surrounded them in the early years of the nineteenth century as their predecessors had been by the dangers and persecutions of the penal code regime of the two preceding ages. More than once have I knelt in the little Friary Chapel at Vesper hour, and listened to the strains of a hymn echoed from the lonely aisles of the adjoining ruined Abbey. Nor could I then fail to be filled with melancholy memories of Meelick's martyred monks in by-gone days, and of its still earlier founders, before Silanchia's ancient glory had departed, or Saxon invaders trod the soil of Erin – before the days of massacre, plunder and confiscation swept over the ill-fated land, sparing neither chief nor peasant, castle or abbey. During the long years of persecution how often may the faithful pilgrims in that ruined church have been surprised at their devotions despite the vigilance of watchful sentinels concealed in the trees, and the pastor and flock mercilessly assailed by the fanatical alien soldiery.

During my pleasant visit and intercourse with the peasantry of the adjoining district, I learned many of its traditions and legends, and was much struck by the accuracy of their statements regarding historical events, some of which I knew to be well authenticated. This was to me all the more surprising as but few of these people could read or write or even speak English well. They pointed out Donal O'Madden's Castle of Cloghan, *on the opposite side of the Shannon and fully detailed its siege by Queen Elizabeth's Lord Deputy, and its brave defence by about two hundred of the O'Madden Sept of Silanchia, all of whom were massacred when the English soldiers took the*

Castle on the 12th March, 1595. They also brought me to the ancient Castle of Lismore, a stronghold of the Chiefs of Silanchia, on the western side of the river about a mile from Meelick Abbey. Many stories they related of the O'Madden race and its warriors; nor were they unmindful of Silanchia's departed heroines, amongst whom were numbered the Lady Mor O'Madden, who died about the year 1320, renowned in song and story for her beauty.

At length my visit to Meelick came to a close on a bright Sunday morning, and I can never forget the scene of my departure. The Friary gates were still crowded with a group of kindly peasants coming forth from the little chapel, as their good pastor, my hospitable host, and aged Friar, of venerable aspect and splendid physique, clasped my hand, exclaiming with impressive earnestness, 'Farewell, probably we may meet no more on earth, but before leaving this Abbey, accept an old priest's blessing, and best wishes, that you and your children's children may unto the end cling to the ancient creed and country for which your forefathers have gave life and property, and retaining that surest sign of predestination – devotion to the Blessed Mother of God – may so prove worthy of their traditions in whatever future God's Providence may have in store for our land.' Whilst I hastened onward to meet the mail coach at Eyrecourt, a fervent aspiration burst from my heart, that long-hoped-for day, when Ireland, with the good will of her sister island, may be in truth described as "Great, glorious and free, fairest flower of the earth, brightest gem of the sea."

As the wheels of the mail coach rattled along over the rough roads leading from the broad flowing Shannon towards the distant metropolis, I sank into a reverie, pondering on the incidents of my sojourn in the West. Before my mind arose the question – can this be the semi-savage people, the ignorant, uncivilised peasantry of whom we have heard so many malignant tongues chatter? Assuredly not. What a contrast do the two nations present – The English yeoman is a great, bold and prosperous people to whom the past or the future are of comparatively little interest, and whose chief aim in life is to secure present comfort and prosperity. And, on the other hand – Ireland's peasantry – the children of a long oppressed race, who, through ages of persecution have still adhered to their ancient faith and traditions, and who, though poverty stricken, are yet hospitable as well as brave, pious, generous and intelligent – a peasantry, moreover, not a few of whom are descendants of ancient families whose fame for sanctity, valour and learning once rang throughout Europe.

During many an after year, and amidst varied scenes in countries far distant where my lot was cast, memories of that old Franciscan Abbey on the Shannon's banks oft arose to my mind. And the Monk of Meelick's blessing clung around and encouraged and cheered me in not a few difficulties and dangers on land and sea.

A decade later, Dr Madden revisited the area of Cloghan castle and Meelick abbey, to heartbreaking evidences of what the locals had endured in the time since his last visit.

Nearly ten years elapsed, when on my return from Australia I again visited Meelick. Oh! What a mournful change has passed over the whole aspect of Ireland within that time! Since I had last seen the Siol Anmchadha famine and pestilence and enforced emigration had devastated the country. In the very district that was once the O'Madden's territory of Silanchia, vix – The Barony of Longford on the west of the Shannon, the population had been reduced to one-half its previous number, or in official figures from 16,893 to 8,609. Whilst in their ancient lands of Lusmagh, on the opposite side of the river, the depopulation was equally appalling.

I travelled for miles along the Shannon valley without meeting a peasant or a cottage with roof left on it, and grass grew over many a once happy homestead. I heard no more the children's merry laughter or the peasant's song; nought anywhere but the wild birds cry or the ravens cawing in the woods – too true was 'The Celt gone – gone with a vengeance' as the newspapers of that day exultingly announced to the world.

The famine of 1846 and following, fever, absentee landlord's vandalism, crowbar evictions, over the land spreading death and desolation on everyman. Between the years of 1846 and 1850, more than a million and a half of Ireland's peasantry were swept away – and the wretched survivors perishing for want of food wandered homeless – thus doomed to die slowly but as surely as if consigned to the gallows or put to the sword. In Meelick Churchyard at rest forever was my old friend the Franciscan Friar, and with him many another Soggarth Aroon, for priests perished with their flocks during the dreadful pestilence of those famine years.

In every part of Ireland I found the same sad state of affairs – heard the same sad story – witnessed the same scenes of irretrievable ruin and destruction caused by the conjoint forces of famine, pestilence and the evictors crowbar brigade. The country towns were de-peopled and poverty stricken. The poor houses and hospitals were crowded beyond their capacity. And, on several occasions I have seen in the ditches the emaciated corpses of some of the evicted tenantry who had wandered away from their roofless homes into the bogs and woods, where they had starved, sickened and died beneath the hedges, their only shelter from the wintry blasts."

In 1990, several churchyards were cleared of undergrowth and tidied up. I stood in one near Cloughjordan and stared in horror at what turned out to be a pit containing so many famine bodies that the ground covering the bones was only a few inches thick. The same sorry sight greeted graveyard clearers in Shinrone in 1991.

Before leaving the famine era in Offaly, I think it would be interesting to quote from two separate recollections. Our first extract is from the memories of William O'Connor Morris. Morris owned Gortnamona, near Blueball, Offaly. He ends a long description of the terrible hardships during the famine with the following words:-

"As regards the Midland Counties, the conduct of the landed gentry was in the main admirable. Rents were not exacted or indeed asked for and arrears were struck off in thousands of cases. The landlords of King's County were not wealthy a class and on many estates they did not possess the means to give employment they gave in the preceeding season. The more opulent however, certainly did so and to this day many works of drainage and planting attest what they then accomplished.

As for my mother and myself we were too poor to imitate examples of this kind but we sold horses and carriages, scarcely thought of rents and happily did not evict a single tenant. My mother too hit on the expedient, useful alike to ourselves and to the poor around us. She sent none of the produce of the home farm to market, but stored it in barns and outhouses and even in the rooms of the house. The drawing room, I recollect, was a granary of oats and she sold it at somewhat less than the current price to our poor dependants and their immediate neighbours.

She rather gained than lost by this kindly conduct and I have thought how well it might have been had the State attempted to do something of the kind in the case of the sensitive Irish people. On the whole, in my experience at least – and it happened to extend over a large district – the upper classes in Ireland did their duty. They made great sacrifices in this season of trial and exhibited sympathy and good feelings as a general rule to the suffering poor and in fact, the divisions which kept them apart from these, were to a considerable extent effaced, in the presence of disasters that appealed to all hearts.

I DWELL ON THIS SUBJECT BECAUSE DESIGNING MEN HAVE OF LATE BEEN DENOUNCING THE IRISH GENTRY AS RECKLESS AND WICKED IN THE FAMINE OF 1846"

William O'Connor Morris died in 1904 and his beautiful house with its fine library was destroyed during the Civil War of 1922-23 as part of the then process of eliminating the desmene lands of local landlords to make them available for a carve up among the land-hungry local men. In the 1930s, as a result of the economic war caused by the actions of a Mr De Valera, land in Ireland dropped in value to £10 per acre and Irishmen and women continued in great numbers to emigrate.

Our second extract concerns the childhood memories of someone whose mother grew up in Cloghan Castle, as the daughter of Garrett Moore. Garrett Moore's daughter grew up, married and became chatelaine of Cahirbane, County Clare. She was affectionately known however as the 'The Lily of Lusmagh'. Her son, who became General Sir O'Moore Creagh VC, GCB, GCSI, dwells in some length, in Chapter 1 of his autobiography, on his early boyhood in County Clare. I include the very many pages of extract that follow, as they do give us an insight into family life in that specific context. I quote:-

"My father, the first of the Creaghs of Cahirbane, County Clare, to take to a sea life, entered the Royal Navy at the age of eleven with the support of Captain (afterwards Admiral Sir Peter) Parker, a friend of my grandfather's. He was engaged on blockade duty on the French coast during the latter part of the Napoleonic Wars, and he was serving in the West Indies when the war with the United States broke out in 1812. He distinguished himself during that campaign in a gunboat action against superior forces; the British fleet was at the time lying becalmed at some distance from land, and he had been sent in command of a tender to procure water ashore. When near the coast he was attacked by two American gunboats carrying heavier guns and larger crews than the tender. His boat could receive no help from the fleet and the choice lay between fighting and surrender. He decided on the former and resisted till his boat was sunk. He was rescued and was interned at New York for the remainder of the struggle, receiving the commendation of the Admiralty for his gallantry. I have often heard him express his gratitude for the kindness with which he was treated by his captors, and especially by the family of the American Commodore, during the time that he was a prisoner of war.

His last active service was at the attack on Algiers in 1816 when he was severely wounded and became incapacitated for further active service. He was appointed to the coast-guard in Ireland on his recovery, and he then married my mother, who was a daughter of Garrett Moore of Cloghan Castle in King's County.

The domain in which the house stands was farmed by my father and consisted of about two hundred and fifty Irish acres of good land, about two miles from the estuary of the River Shannon, and streams flowed through it into the great river, which here is tidal and several miles wide. They abounded in fish and wild fowl, while wild duck bred on their banks. There was splendid fishing and shooting almost outside the door; in hard winters I have killed snipe in the farm-yard. There was a pack of harriers close by, and one of the best packs of fox-hounds in Ireland was kennelled twelve miles away in the county of Limerick. It was a glorious country to live in those days; it abounded in country seats, mostly inhabited by our relatives, and there was plenty of society. A neighbouring country gentleman, on his death-bed when nearly eighty years old, was consolingly told by the parson that he was going to a better land, but replied doubtingly: "I have lived, man and boy, for over seventy years in Balnagarde and it takes a lot of bating" (beating).

"I was born at Cahirbane in April 1848, the eighth child of a family of nine sons and two daughters (one of my brothers died before I was born and one sister when I was too young to recall her), and three of my brothers were younger than I. In my childhood I saw little of my eldest brother, who was at school till he went to the Royal Military College, and in 1854 got his commission in the 1st Royals, then at the seat of war in the Crimea. He came home for a short leave before joining and I well recollect his departure and how I envied him. During his short stay at home, he practised sword exercise daily before an admiring audience of grooms, stable boys and other hangers-on, then

extremely numerous in our house. A broomstick was set up in the farm-yard for him to practise on, and when he made a good cut he was greeted by approving shouts of 'Arrah, look boys! Tis himself will clip off the heads of the Roosians in fine style.'

"We younger children regarded our father with the greatest awe; we were only allowed into his presence on state occasions such as dinner-parties, when we were dressed up in our best clothes, solemnly marched into the dining-room during dessert, presented to the guests and to our father, who gave us each a wine-glass of whisky-punch and some sweets. After swallowing them, we withdrew with equal solemnity, which was only abandoned when we got outside the dining room door and fell on the good things in the still-room, fighting for them, as the old butler used to say, "like a pack of fox-hounds".

Whisky was the universal panacea for all the ills of life. When we children suffered from an inward pain we were given a lump of sugar soaked in it. After our hair was cut our heads were well rubbed with it as a prophylactic against cold. We were very wild and shy in the company of strangers and found not a little difficulty in comporting ourselves correctly when taken into society. Our child visitors, always relegated to the schoolroom, found the ordeal as trying as we did… Our schoolroom was a merry one. My dear mother made its care her special business, for her children were her greatest joy. We loved her and her will was our law as long as she lived. She died over thirty-five years ago, aged about eighty-four. In her youth she had been very beautiful; she had a clear pink and white complexion, jet black hair, Irish blue-violet eyes and a perfect figure. She rode straight to hounds, and was an accomplished musician with a charming voice, singing Irish ballads with exquisite feeling and accompanying herself on the harp or guitar. She was very popular, especially among my father's tenantry, who called her 'The Lily of Lusmagh', the name of the barony in which Cloghan Castle is situated. She often sang and played in our schoolroom, and on such occasions, the servants and hangers-on used to be admitted, much to their delight.

Our system of education in early youth was admirably adapted to the requirements of the profession of arms for which we were destined from our birth. To even think of adopting any other, of which we were never guilty, would have been regarded as unworthy of the family traditions. Our tutor was the son of a neighbouring farmer, who, not being a man of "quality", treated us with the greatest respect; he was well educated in classical and Irish lore and in mathematics. A dancing master appeared periodically, attended by his son (an ex-sergeant of artillery) as fiddler. Their visits lasted about three weeks at a time. The method of teaching us jig-steps was peculiar. The dancing master tied a straw rope, called in Irish, "sugan", round one leg of a pupil, and a withy)ordinarily used to bind the twigs of a broom together, and called in Irish a "gad") round the pupil's other leg. The fiddler would then strike up a tune and his father would shout directions for our movements in a stentorian voice: "Rise upon sugan, sink upon gad". "Gad, gad, sugan, gad", and so on. The dancing master used to get excited, and so did his son, and the longer the step-drill lasted, the quicker was played the tune and the more violent became the exercise. There was generally an audience who joined in, and the fun then became fast and furious.

An old ex-Captain, a sort of Dugald Dalgety, who had served in two or three South American armies, occupied the honorary position of superintendent of studies. He was a clever, well-educated man, who knew French and Latin perfectly, and spoke them with the strongest Irish brogue that I have ever heard, and he was deeply read in ancient and in modern history He used to tell us vivid stories of his campaigns, and he used to end up by remarking that the passions and the mental qualities of the races of mankind are little changed by time and that they produce very similar effects from age to age so that the political problems which arise are much the same at all periods of the world's history. We loved to listen to him, and subsequent experiences have convinced me that his views on human psychology were correct. From time to time he reported progress to our father, and he pronounced us to be clever – on what grounds I do not know, and I do not think that he knew himself.

The tutor, however, we voted a bore and we absented ourselves from our studies when we thought fit; nor were we ever called to account for it. We ran wild among the peasantry, camping out in the bogs and woods, snaring birds, catching fish and poaching. Our peasant companions filled our heads with legends and stories of the ancient glories of our race, which we firmly believed and so became filled with racial pride. We often went about bare-footed and, like wild things, were perfectly happy. Visitors, such as our attorney or as some steward from an outlying farm, occasionally arrived, whose social position was too high for the servants' hall but was not high enough for admission amongst the quality, and such people were entertained in the school-room. They, their peculiarities and their stories always interested us; our sense of hospitality compelled us to treat them with attention, and this further interfered with our studies. I learnt little in early life from books but learnt much from nature and from association with all sorts and conditions of men. This taught me sympathy with the wants, failings and aspirations of others. I moreover developed a good constitution, which has stood me in good stead in the bad climates in which my lot was sometimes to be cast.

It is interesting, today when they have disappeared, to recall some of the time-honoured customs which prevailed in my native county in the middle of the last century. In those days the peasantry revered the ancient county families, most of which have since that time left the country. The peasantry called a country gentleman's residence the "Big House", and they always alluded to its owner and to his wife as "Himself" and "Herself". It was the usual custom for certain of the families of the tenants to provide the domestic servants for the Big House, and also the artisans for the estate and the labourers needed for the home farm – as they had been doing for generations. When one of these retainers became old and feeble, he or she was allowed to introduce a young relative as an assistant or, when ill, as a substitute. No retainer was ever sent adrift.

The domestic servants looked upon themselves almost as relatives of the owner of the Big House and of the family which they served, with which they always maintained a friendly if respectful, intimacy. They regarded its honour as their own, and there was nothing that they would not do to uphold it. They at the same time assumed a right, which was not often disputed, to have a "say" in matters affecting the general welfare, and they passively resisted all innovations; for innovations of all kinds they hated. Our old home, for instance, possesses no bath-room, so baths, if required, had to be carried up to the bedrooms. We children got these when we could, but when they were not provided we, both in summer and in winter, resorted to a stream which ran close by the house. However, my eldest brother, after being for a time in England, insisted upon having a hip-bath in his bedroom every morning, and we all followed suit. This innovation our old butler strenuously resisted for a time; but eventually he gave way, remarking, "Troth, an ye must be dirty divils to want such a power of washing". The old man, who had filled the position for over fifty years, used to chip into the conversation when attending at dinner if he happened to be particularly interested in anything that was said either by "Himself" or by some guest.

As servants were seldom discharged, establishments were always far too large and included a number of hangers-on; but there was little employment elsewhere and wages were very low, which was not an unmixed evil. Although the servants were not lazy, their work was apt to be incomplete and in the Irish phrase "through other".

Marriages amongst the peasantry generally took place at a very early age; the bridegroom would usually be eighteen and the bride sixteen. This custom was encouraged by the priests. As these newly-married couples seldom possessed any means of subsistence individually, they had to be given a potato patch of about a couple of acres' extent by their parents; and as a result of this system, farms had come from such continual sub-division to be too small to provide a living for their occupants. The servants of Big Houses were usually given a potato patch of somewhat larger dimensions by "Himself", together with a comparatively decent cottage; their mode of life was, in consequence, somewhat more civilized than that of other peasants, to whom they set a good example and one which was not without some effect.

But although the peasantry, for the most part, may be said to have existed almost in a state of semi-starvation, this did not affect their natural cheerfulness of disposition. Rustic entertainments were constantly in full swing and consisted of dances, donkey races and hurling matches on Sundays after Mass. The dances usually took place at cross-roads where there was a forge, the door of which was unhinged and used as a platform for jig-dancing. The music was provided by an itinerant fiddler or piper, who was paid a halfpenny each by dancers and the most affluent of the audience. The smith never objected; no one touched his tools, for a forge was regarded with the greatest veneration.

For the donkey races "Himself" usually gave a prize of a collar and hames, or some other piece of harness. Hurling matches often ended in a free fight, which added to the day's enjoyment. On St John's Day in June, bonfires were lit on certain hills; the peasants assembled around them and engaged in sham fights armed with lighted sheaves of straw. On St Stephen's Day, the peasants hunted the wren, after which they assembled and held a sort of carnival at the Big House, when "Himself" gave them whisky to drink his health. St Patrick's Day was one of merriment accompanied by much whisky drinking. When a few people met, the one who first said, "My Patrick's pot on you" was entitled to a drink of whisky from the others.

There were also wakes when much whisky and tobacco were consumed, and when old women mourned for the deceased with shrill cries, interrupted periodically by stories in praise of his virtues and those of his family. These old women were called keeners, from the Gaelic work cuineadh *which means mourning and is pronounced keena. Faction fights were of frequent occurrence; the peasants all belonged to some warring faction or another; the quarrels had usually originated in ancient days and the subject of the dispute had long been forgotten. Rival factions met by appointment, usually on some racecourse after the races were over, and engaged in combat with one another armed with sticks called* shillalaghs. *The fights often resulted in deaths and serious injuries, but the combatants, none the less on that account, enjoyed themselves vastly.*

Gaelic was generally spoken by the peasantry in our remote corner of Clare at that time. But it became a dead language in later years until, in the early 'nineties, the ancient language was revived amongst some of the Anglo-Irish by one Douglas Hyde, whose name seems to indicate his race. As I was naturally quick at picking up dialects, I spoke Gaelic as a child, but I have long since almost totally forgotten it. It may be recalled that the late Lord Wolseley, by way of encouraging officers linguistic studies, told them that a facility in acquiring languages was a fool's accomplishment, and I sometimes wonder if he was right. Another Irishman, Lord Palmerston, when informed that somebody could speak six different foreign tongues fluently, remarked: "Has he ever said anything worth hearing in any one of them?"

There were still left in Ireland in my early youth some of the class called Scanachaide (anglice shanachie), *meaning antiquary, who were successors to the bards of old. They have long since finally disappeared from the land, and the ancient legends and the folklore of the Gaels have to a great extent disappeared with them, but their songs and their stories inspired copious literature written in English. The profession of shanachie was hereditary, and as these people were quite illiterate their lore was passed on verbally from father to son. They were very poor, and they wandered about ragged and bare-footed, being freely entertained both in the servants' hall of the Big House and in the peasants' cabins. Their songs and stories were rather of the Oriental type, songs and stores that sparkled with imagination of a far-fetched nature and that were usually in the last degree pathetic, treating of the deeds of devotion and the sufferings of the Irish-Gaelic race in the past. The peasants loved to listen to them, and as a child, my pleasure in hearing them was equally great. But the shanachies inculcated an unwholesome rare conceit and false ideas of chivalry, and they, in consequence, contributed in no small degree to bringing about the disturbed state of the country. This was especially the case when they held up land-owning families of recent origin, or families descended from sequestrators who had gained possession of confiscated estates, to contempt. They would point to a person of old race (even then a rare avis outside of a few remote spots) as the real owner of the land occupied by the "Saxon" owner, whose Big House nothing would induce a shanachie to visit.*

The race conceit, the whimsical sentimentality and the extreme particularism which now prevail amongst the Irish peasantry are largely due to English literature, inspired by the songs and the stories of the shanachies. To this, and to talk about "self-determination", the development of the present revolutionary and republican movement in Ireland may be traced. Napoleon said with great truth, "C'est l'imagination qui domine le monde". *Nine-tenths of the inhabitants of Ireland nowadays are of English, Scotch or Welsh descent, * and there is no* "Irish Nation" distinct from the British nation. * As borne out by DNA testing

The shanachies, it should be mentioned, related the legends that are attached to almost every ruined castle, and these castles were numerous, and also the legends attached to each rath and conspicuous hill. They knew, or affected to know, the pedigree of every ancient family in the countryside, and they would tell of the ban-sigh (pronounced banshee) *or fairy-woman, whose cries announced the death of one of the family's members. They would give the fairy's reason for attaching herself to a particular family, which generally concluded with: "They were a great people, some were hanged, some were transported, but they were never beaten, and always took revenge sooner or later". Holy wells abounded, and these the peasants were wont to visit when ill; bringing as offering some trifle – usually a bit of broken crockery or even an old rag – to the patron saint ensured a cure.*

The peasants' cabins were too wretched to be dignified by the name of cottages. They were built of mud, and were so miserably thatched that many were not rainproof and consisted of one room only; the exit for the smoke from the fireplace was often merely a hole in the roof. Sanitary arrangements did not exist. The peasants had few blankets or bedsteads; they usually slept on straw spread on the earthen floor and possessed nothing in the shape of furniture except a rough wooden table, a wooden bench or two, a dresser on which to lay their few pieces of crockery kept for ornament not use, and a large metal pot in which to boil the potatoes that, together with water, were their only diet for the greater part of the year. In summer milk or butter-milk was substituted for water, and mushrooms were added as a relish to the potatoes. Their only luxuries were newly-distilled whisky, called poteen – made in illicit stills – and tobacco of a very rank kind, which was sold at four shillings and eightpence a pound and burnt so slowly that a pipeful provided several smokes. On festive occasions, including wakes, the guests drank to excess, but the peasantry were not habitual drunkards.

Land was necessary to subsistence, and land-hunger raged. Many landlords let their lands to middlemen who sublet to the cultivators for exorbitant rent. Happy was the peasant who owned a sow, which was fed chiefly on the skins of the potatoes left after the family meal; it shared the cabin with the family and it helped to pay the rent. The only relief from these miserable conditions was emigration; and it entailed severe hardships, for many of those who at this time quitted their native land knew only the Gaelic language, and these, especially the young women, suffered cruel adversity on arrival in a foreign country.

My father never had any trouble with his people, to whom he was always accessible and sympathetic, for he was liked and respected by them because he was one of the ancient race. He understood them and he dealt with them in accordance with customs handed down from former times. This would have been resented had he not been one of "the old stock". He was most conservative, managed his estates himself, never tolerated the intervention of a middleman, and was a kind and considerate landlord who often forgot his rights but who never forgot the duties that he owed to his tenantry. Although on the Grand Jury and Justice of the Peace, he was a law unto himself in dealing with his own people, and this greatly added to his popularity".

- The Autobiography of General Sir O'moore Creagh, VC, GCB, GCSI

Chapter 13

The Moores of Shannon Grove and the Catholic Bishop who got Married

The Moores of Shannon Grove and the Catholic Bishop who got married

Some 200 years ago, the younger brother of Garrett Moore of Cloghan Castle (who called himself The O'Moore and who died in 1824) was called John Hubert Moore of Anaghbeg.

He built himself a house on the banks of the River Shannon near Meelick, on land which I think had been in the family for hundreds of years. He called his house "Shannon Grove" and some 100 years later it was to be the home of a Mr and Mrs Waller who were grandparents of our very good friend, Valerie Landon.

John Hubert fell in love with a young lady called Maria Butler from Killoskehane Castle, near Borrisoleigh in County Tipperary.

It so happens that this castle was owned by some other very good friends of ours who came from America. Many happy times had we spent in their delightful home which had a fine collection of furniture made for the building by the Butlers.

Maria's father, Theobald, was descended from the 2nd or 11th Baron Dunboyne (a cadet of the Earls of Ormond). He was a distant relative of 12th or 22nd Baron Dunboyne.

This latter Dunboyne was a Roman Catholic Bishop who felt it his duty, on his inheritance of the title, to produce a son and heir.

He resigned his bishopric but his Primate refused to release him from his priestly vows so he wrote to Pope Pious V. Unfortunately, his dispensation was not forthcoming, and now well advanced in years he became impatient.

He arranged a marriage with Maria Butler, who immediately laid plans for an elopement with John Moore during the course of the hunt. Unfortunately, her father became suspicious and removed her to another property to forestall her plans. Lord Dunboyne obviously panicked and married her at once in an Anglican Church. He was immediately excommunicated and the Irish Bishops vowed not to receive him back into the Catholic Church "until the waters ran backwards". The papal correspondence on the subject was couched in very strong language.

The marriage lasted 14 years and produced only one stillborn daughter. Maria was said to have been a loyal wife. John Hubert Moore married but his wife died.

The now Anglican ex-Bishop desired in his declining years to be re-admitted to the Catholic Church but since bribery from excommunicants is forbidden by Canon law and the waters showed no signs of flowing backwards, he was unable to do so. On 2nd May 1800, some five days before his death, Lord Dunboyne appealed to the Pope. Lady Dunboyne gave orders that no priest was to be admitted to their house in Leeson Street, Dublin. It is said that two friars (one of them was a Father Graham) gained entry disguised as doctors and reduced him to tears. They then hoisted him by his feet until tears trickled back into his eyes. Thus, the waters were deemed to have reversed their normal progress. The priests now considered themselves released from the vow of the bishops and identified themselves. They received him back into the church, administered absolution and prevailed upon him to alter his will in favour of the church. They left the house without revealing their true identities to the suspicious family. The funeral was conducted in the utmost secrecy and Lord Dunboyne's servants (accompanied by his widow) arrived at the Augustinian Priory in Fethard, County Tipperary one snowy day in May and armed with swords and pistols guarded his tomb.

Lengthy litigation followed the publication of his will, when it was discovered that the Dunboyne Castle Estate had been bequeathed to St Patrick's Catholic College, Maynooth. His widow did not commence the litigation but his Catholic sister did so, on the grounds that the Roman Catholic Church forbade converts to Catholicism to bequeath property on a deathbed conversion. When called upon to give evidence, Father Graham refused, pleading the seal of the confessional. He and his colleague were promptly jailed for contempt of court.

Eventually, a private settlement was obtained by a special Act of Parliament wherein the integrity of the estate was respected subject to an annuity of £500 to the College. Maria got the Leeson Street house and £1,200 per annum. This was a huge sum of money in those days.

Eighteen months later, she married her first love John Hubert Moore and went to live in Shannon Grove. They had a son, Hubert Butler Moore, who died in 1873, a descendant of whom was Pamela Wood, one-time owner of Cloghan Castle. John Hubert Moore had a son by his first wife, who was Colonel Hans Garrett Moore, noted for his bravery in the Crimean War and father of Colonel Hans Garrett Moore, VC.

Maria died on 6th August 1860 aged 95 years and she is buried in the Moore tomb in the front of Clonfert Cathedral.

Chapter 14

The Graves Family

The Graves Family

The Graves And Their Banker Tenants

Robert James Graves

A new era of Cloghan Castle dawned with the coming of Dr. Robert Graves in 1852. He was one of the founders of modern clinical medicine and the discoverer of Graves Disease (of the thyroid).

Dr. Robert James Graves was descended from Colonel Graves, who commanded a regiment of cavalry in Cromwell's army, and, having settled in Ireland, acquired considerable landed property in the County of Limerick.

Dr Graves' father, Richard Graves (the son of the first wife of my great grandfather Dr. Charles Donovan) had a distinguished undergraduate career in Trinity College, taking a scholarship in 1782, and winning numerous prizes. He took Holy Orders and became a Fellow of T.C.D. in 1796, and subsequently was appointed Dean of Ardagh. His literary works (of which twenty-seven have been collected and published in four volumes) are of a high order of merit, and he acquired great celebrity for his lectures on the 'Pentateuch.' He married Eliza, daughter of James Drought, D.D., Professor of Divinity, T.C.D., and a member of an ancient family in the King's County.

In the summer of 1992, we had a visit from Australia by the great-great grandson of Dr. Graves. Having spoken with Dr Graves's descendants over the years, I am grateful for the following information (and I am told that more information can be found in *The Graves Family in Ireland*, by Jim Cooke.)

> *Robert James, was born on the 27th March 1797, in Dublin. He was educated, first by the Rev. Ralph Wilde (who in 1782 had won a scholarship in Trinity College), and, secondly, by Mr. Levey, a well-known teacher. Having entered Trinity College, he passed through an undergraduate course, in which he almost rivalled his father. At his entrance he took first place, and in all his subsequent examinations save two he won the first premium. On taking his Fellow Commoner's degree he received the gold medal for having entered for every examination open to him, and obtaining a valde in omnibus. In 1815 he graduated in Arts, becoming an M.B. in 1818 and a M.D. in 1841.*
>
> *Having decided upon medicine as his profession, he studied in every department of it with the utmost ardour, not confining himself to School of Physics, but working also in the College School. He early recognised the importance of morbid anatomy to the pathologist, and never neglected the opportunities for extending his knowledge of disease, which post mortem examination offered. The*

*years 1818, 1819 and 1820, were spent by Graves studying in foreign universities. During two years he was a pupil of Professor Stromeyer and Blumenbach, of Gottingen, and of Hufeland and Behrend, of Berlin. In Copenhagen, he studied under the eminent Professor Cohlston. During his sojourn on the Continent, he met with many adventures.**

*[*The late Dr. Stokes recounts the following one:- 'He had embarked at Genoa, in a brig bound for Sicily. The captain and crew were Sicilians, and there were no passengers on board but himself and a poor Spaniard, who became his companion and messmate. Soon after quitting the land, they encountered a terrific gale from the northeast, with which the ill-found, ill-mannered, and badly commanded vessel, soon showed herself unable to contend. The sails were blown away or torn, the vessel was leaking, the pumps choked, and the crew in despair gave up the attempt to work the ship. At this juncture Graves was lying on a couch in the cabin, suffering under a painful malady, when his fellow-passenger entered, and in terror announced to him that the crew were about to forsake the vessel; the two passengers were to be left to their fate. Springing from his couch, Graves flung on his cloak, and, looking through the cabin, found a heavy axe lying on the floor. This he seized, and concealing it under his cloak he gained the deck, and found that the captain and crew had nearly succeeded in getting the boat free from its lashings. He addressed the captain, declaring his opinion that the boat could not live in such a sea, and that the attempt to launch it was madness. He was answered by an execration, and told that it was a matter with which he had nothing to do, for that he and his companion should remain behind. "Then", said he, "if that be the case, let us all be drowned together – it is a pity to part good company." As he spoke, he struck the sides of the boat with his axe, and destroyed it irreparably. The captain drew his dagger, and would have rushed upon him, but quailed before the cool, erect and unarmed man. Graves then virtually took command of the ship. He had the suckers of the pumps withdrawn, and furnished by cutting from his own boots the leather necessary to repair the valves, the crew returned to their duties, the leak was gained, and the vessel saved.]*

On one occasion he was confined for ten days in a dungeon in an Austrian prison on a charge of being a spy. His assertion that he was an Englishman was disregarded on the ground that only a German could speak such excellent English as he did! Whilst travelling in Italy he formed a friendship with the great artist Turner; Graves himself possessed considerable artistic skill, and many admirable sketches from nature, which he made, are extant. Having spent a few months in Edinburgh, Graves settled in Dublin in 1821 and was in the same year appointed Physician to the Meath Hospital, and at once commenced that system of clinical – i.e. bedside teaching which was destined ere long to render himself and his hospital famous throughout medical circles, even far beyond the boundaries of the British Isles.

In 1824, Graves joined with others in establishing the Park Street School and was its first lecturer on medical jurisprudence. He also lectured in it upon 'Animal Chemistry', a department of the science at that time in its infancy. He was so thoroughly practical as a teacher that, not content with merely lecturing upon toxicology and animal chemistry, he made the following announcement in his syllabus – 'In order to give the students an opportunity of becoming practically acquainted with this part of the subject, they will be allowed to perform all experiments themselves, under the direction of DOCTOR GRAVES.'

Graves now began to acquire a good practice, which, however, never was as large as Cheyne's; and it is remarkable that it decreased somewhat during the latter part of his life, not because he was becoming too old (for he died in the prime of life) but for some reasons difficult to understand. One of the greatest physicians, not alone of Ireland, but of Europe – many practitioners who never put forth an original idea have had larger clienteles – still Graves had many patients, and for some time his practice was undoubtedly large.

On the 27th November 1820, Graves obtained the Licence of the College of Physicians, was elected a Fellow on the 7th April 1823, and in 1843 and 1844 filled the Presidential Chair of the College.

In 1827 Graves was appointed Professor of the institutes of medicine in the School of Physio – an office that he held until 1848. In that year he withdrew from professional work, and two years later resigned his position in the Meath Hospital, but remained until his death Consulting Physician to the Adelaide and the Coombe Hospitals and St. Peter's Parish Dispensary. He was one of the principal founders of the Pathological Society, and their first President, retaining the Presidency for many years. This Society was the first of the kind in the United Kingdom. In 1849 Graves was elected a Fellow of the Royal Society. His wife presented his bust, in marble, executed by his countryman, John Hogan, to the College of Physicians, and his statue, sculptured by Bruce Joy, adorns one of the College Halls. Bruce Joy is the son of the late Dr. William Hunt Joy, an Irishman and a Fellow of the College of Physicians.

Dr. Graves married Anna, daughter of the Rev. William Grogan of Slaney Park, Rector of Baltinglass. They had two sons and four daughters; one of the former was a clergyman, and the other a Lieutenant Colonel in the 83rd Regiment.

After a protracted illness, enduring with remarkable patience, Graves died from disease of the liver on the 28th March 1853, aged fifty-six, and was interred in Mount Jerome Cemetery.

His widow gave up her house in Merrion Square, Dublin and came to live in Cloghan Castle. The Graves were a very distinguished family related to Robert Graves the writer and poet, but I do find it very difficult to understand the Doctor's widow. The taxation system imposed from England was totally unsuitable in Ireland because it levied considerable taxes on the landlords for houses occupied by tenants who could not afford to pay rent. It was this tax, which caused the ruin of many landlords. The new landlords who came to the land after the famine and the sale of bankrupt estates were seldom merciful and mostly Irish. The Cloghan Castle estate was by this time reduced to 1,500 acres and Mrs. Graves evicted a number of non-rent paying tenants.

Dr. Graves had bequeathed a gift of £30,000 worth of books to Trinity College, Dublin. This was a huge fortune in those days. It therefore becomes all the more difficult to understand the eviction of 100 families from their worthless cottages by his widow. She was the daughter of a clergyman and the widow of one of this country's most famous of dedicated doctors. I don't know how she could live with herself, but her actions led to a life surrounded by policemen as her tenants tried to shorten her days and left a legacy of bitter, bitter memories which I hope will now be expunged in a new and prosperous Ireland. In defence of Mrs. Graves, one should not overlook the facts that (a) she was a woman running the estate on her own (b) she had an unwanted village (c) that village paid no rent to her (d) she paid taxes on those dwellings.

A more long-sighted landlord would have offered the inhabitants something else and thus not left a legacy of problems brought on by the hostilities she needlessly created. Famine and eviction were the horrors of Irish history which have led to the type of 'warfare' we see today in Northern Ireland. This has a long pedigree, but it is the same genre repeated over the centuries. I was fortunate to borrow a copy of the book *Crowned Harp* by Nora Robertson, which again, displays a perfect time capsule in Chapter Three as follows:

Florence Graves

'My mother, Florence, the youngest child of Dr. Robert Graves, FRS, was a born radical. How it came about I do not know. Her most conventional and decorous mother, Anna, coming from a country family, it was a constant irritant to my grandmother that her husband was a doctor. She worked the eminence to which he rose so adroitly that the Lord Lieutenant and his lady actually dined with them in Merrion Square. Still, she could not feel that his 'imprimatur' was as enduring as founding a country seat and, before his death, she persuaded him to buy Cloghan Castle, a distinctive Norman Keep by the Shannon, near Banagher. I am very glad she did as its proximity to Birr led later to my parents' meeting.

My grandfather Robert Graves was born in 1796, before the Battle of the Nile and the Irish Rebellion. Between us, we span an alarming stretch of history because my mother was born only shortly before his death in 1853 and I appeared latish in her marriage. Robert, who was a Fellow of the Royal Society, was the Doctor who gave his name to the disease. His statue is in the Hall of the College of Physicians, facing his great contemporary, Sir Williams Stokes, PRCP.

The Anglo-Irish are so much associated with landlordism, great and small, that a chronicle of their more social and cultural activities provides a humane alternative field. The Cromwellian settlement introduced many families who later obtained real eminence drawn from a different social order from that of most of those of Elizabethan and Stuart origins.

Robert Graves did not long survive as a semi-country gentleman and after his death, in 1853, my grandmother left Dublin and moved down to Cloghan Castle with "Little Flo", ten years younger than any of her other children.

My mother's account of those days included: reading the classics in the worst of light concealed under heavy furniture; of the sound of the maid's vanishing footsteps down the stone spiral steps from the attic bedroom where she was crying herself to sleep from fright; of the happy Sunday breakfasts when, instead of plain 'stir-about', she was allowed the treat – of the top of her mother's boiled egg. The rest was policemen. Kind R.I.C. constables were her playmates at bird's-nesting and helping her to ride. Her mother was a harsh landlord and therefore, under constant 'protection'. My mother, no doubt mindful of the egg top, was fond of the hard, beautiful little woman and hoped that she would not be shot; but even then, felt that if she were, she richly deserved it.

Her recollection of the poverty in those post-famine years was distressing, but she formed an affection for the people which never left her, though subsequently it was overlaid by social life in Dublin, and after that as a gunner's pretty wife in garrison towns. Her favourite relatives were Graves's cousins and, I think, of these Robert, the friend and biographer of Rowan Hamilton, influenced her taste in literature.

Her mother had no intellectual interests, but a nice taste in objects d'art (sic). The learned Graves family, whose marriages were still enlarging their cultural scope, disparaged her as a worldly ignoramus.

The recollection, which formed the deepest aversion in my mother's young mind, was the intensive evangelical and Anti-Roman atmosphere of that day. It had degenerated from its early fire to smouldering embers of intolerance. Well-to-do old ladies collected together, abusing their neighbours and puffing up their own worth as "happy, saved Christians, dear". Naturally many evangelicals led saintly lives, including my mother's elder brother Richard, who was in Orders in England.

Shortly after my mother grew up, her mother died and Cloghan Castle was passed to her brother William, who had two sons. The elder and godly Richard had died leaving an only daughter, but to my grandmother's ambition the male line mattered most and Richard's daughter was passed over. She married into the family of J.M. Synge.

Beyond being an army racquets champion, William has left nothing for his family to remember; his two very nice sons died and eventually, William's widow sold Cloghan Castle. At the auction, my mother bought a huge 'famille verte' bowl, looted from the Imperial Palace at Peking, which a grateful patient had given to Robert Graves. It is the only souvenir I have of my grandfather and it now roosts where I write.'

The estate was sold in 1908 to the Land Commission who reduced the castle demesne to under 200 acres.

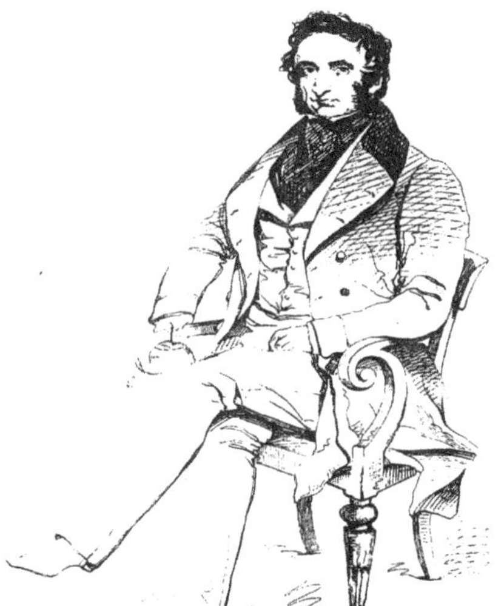

Dr Robert Graves, seated. Credit: Royal College of Physicians of Ireland

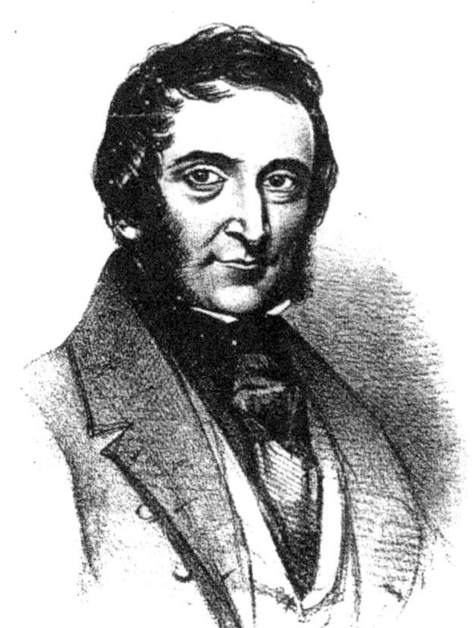

Dr Robert Graves, portrait. Credit: Royal College of Physicians of Ireland

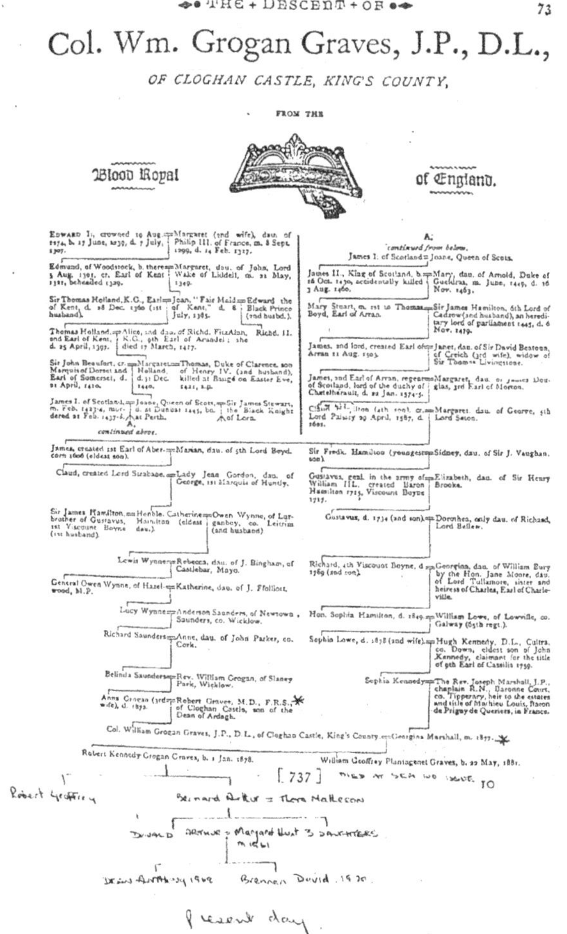

THE DESCENT OF 73

Col. Wm. Grogan Graves, J.P., D.L.,

OF CLOGHAN CASTLE, KING'S COUNTY,

FROM THE

Blood Royal of England.

EDWARD I., crowned 19 Aug. 1274, b. 17 June, 1239, d. 7 July, 1307. = Margaret (2nd wife), dau. of Philip III. of France, m. 8 Sept. 1299, d. 14 Feb. 1317.

Edmund, of Woodstock, b. there 5 Aug. 1301, cr. Earl of Kent 1321, beheaded 1329. = Margaret, dau. of John, Lord Wake of Liddell, m. 21 May, 1349.

Sir Thomas Holland, K.G., Earl of Kent, d. 28 Dec. 1360 (1st husband). = Joan, "Fair Maid of Kent," d. 8 July, 1385. = Edward the Black Prince (2nd husbd.).

Thomas Holland, 2nd Earl of Kent, d. 25 April, 1397. = Alice, 2nd dau. of Richd. FitzAlan, K.G., 9th Earl of Arundel; she died 17 March, 1417. Richd. II.

Sir John Beaufort, cr. Marquis of Dorset and Earl of Somerset, d. 21 April, 1410. = Margaret Holland, d. 31 Dec. 1440. = Thomas, Duke of Clarence, son of Henry IV. (2nd husband), killed at Baugé on Easter Eve, 1421, s.p.

James I. of Scotland, m. Feb. 1423-4, murdered 21 Feb. 1437-8. = Joane, Queen of Scots, d. at Dunbar 1445, bu. at Perth. = Sir James Stewart, the Black Knight of Lorn.

A. *continued above.*

A. *continued from below.*

James I. of Scotland = Joane, Queen of Scots.

James II., King of Scotland, b. 16 Oct. 1430, accidentally killed 3 Aug. 1460. = Mary, dau. of Arnold, Duke of Gueldres, m. June, 1449, d. 16 Nov. 1463.

Mary Stuart, m. 1st to Thomas Boyd, Earl of Arran. = Sir James Hamilton, 6th Lord of Cadzow (2nd husband), an hereditary lord of parliament 1445, d. 6 Nov. 1479.

James, 2nd lord, created Earl of Arran 11 Aug. 1503. = Janet, dau. of Sir David Beatoun, of Creich (3rd wife), widow of Sir Thomas Livingstone.

James, 2nd Earl of Arran, regent of Scotland, lord of the duchy of Chatelherault, d. 22 Jan. 1574-5. = Margaret, dau. of James Douglas, 3rd Earl of Morton.

Claud Hamilton (4th son), cr. Lord Paisley 29 April, 1587, d. 1621. = Margaret, dau. of George, 5th Lord Seton.

James, created 1st Earl of Abercorn 1606 (eldest son). = Marian, dau. of 5th Lord Boyd.

Sir Fredk. Hamilton (youngest son). = Sidney, dau. of Sir J. Vaughan.

Claud, created Lord Strabane. = Lady Jean Gordon, dau. of George, 1st Marquis of Huntly.

Gustavus, genl. in the army of William III., created Baron Hamilton 1715, Viscount Boyne 1717. = Elizabeth, dau. of Sir Henry Brooke.

Sir James Hamilton, brother of Gustavus, 1st Viscount Boyne (1st husband). = Honble. Catherine Hamilton (eldest dau.) = Owen Wynne, of Lurganboy, co. Leitrim (2nd husband).

Gustavus, d. 1734 (2nd son). = Dorothea, only dau. of Richard, Lord Bellew.

Lewis Wynne = Rebecca, dau. of J. Bingham, of Castlebar, Mayo.

Richard, 4th Viscount Boyne, d. 1789 (2nd son). = Georgina, dau. of William Bury by the Hon. Jane Moore, dau. of Lord Tullamore, sister and heiress of Charles, Earl of Charleville.

General Owen Wynne, of Hazelwood, M.P. = Katherine, dau. of J. Ffolliott.

Lucy Wynne = Anderson Saunders, of Newtown Saunders, co. Wicklow.

Hon. Sophia Hamilton, d. 1849. = William Lowe, of Lowville, co. Galway (65th regt.).

Richard Saunders = Anne, dau. of John Parker, co. Cork.

Sophia Lowe, d. 1878 (2nd wife). = Hugh Kennedy, D.L., Cultra, co. Down, eldest son of John Kennedy, claimant for the title of 9th Earl of Cassilis 1759.

Belinda Saunders = Rev. William Grogan, of Slaney Park, Wicklow.

Sophia Kennedy = The Rev. Joseph Marshall, J.P., chaplain R.N., Baronne Court, co. Tipperary, heir to the estates and title of Mathieu Louis, Baron de Prigny de Queriers, in France.

Anna Grogan (3rd wife), d. 1893. = Robert Graves, M.D., F.R.S., of Cloghan Castle, son of the Dean of Ardagh. *

Col. William Grogan Graves, J.P., D.L., of Cloghan Castle, King's County = Georgina Marshall, m. 1877. *

Robert Kennedy Grogan Graves, b. 1 Jan. 1878.

William Geoffrey Plantagenet Graves, b. 22 May, 1881.

[737]

Robert Geoffrey

Present day

Graves Family Tree

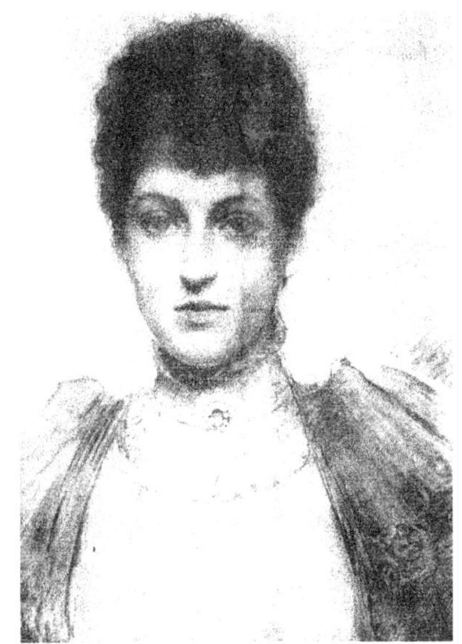

Mrs Georgina Graves

Mrs Georgina Graves, wife of Lt Col William Graves JP DL, who later married a Mr Barton after the death of Colonel Graves. She is remembered with much affection locally and every Christmas had a party for the children of Lusmagh school.

Buried Gold

Taken from a press cutting from the *'Kings County Chronicle'*, dated 17th March 1892:

'There are fewer places around Birr that can be visited with greater interest than this historic castellated pile now, and we hope long to be, occupied by Captain Wright, master and owner of two packs of Hounds and Harriers, who has won great popularity, and also his friend and companion Englishman, Mr. Thomas Craddock, since they came here.

To begin, the castle though not so rich in warlike and dreaded deeds in the medieval times as Leap Castle, has not weird ghosts stories of bygone days, and creaking doors, and moaning banshees to add to its otherwise strange and eventful story, is still full of romantic associations. From its summit, a splendid view is obtained of the surrounding country, and the whole of Lusmagh lies as it were at the spectator's feet, with the Little Brosna running through it like a silver streak.

Capt. Wright, who is an English gentleman, rented the property from the representatives of the late Col. Grogan Graves and he maintains a very large hunting establishment. In short, he came over from England chiefly for hunting, being an out-and-out lover of the chase. His two packs – The County Galway Foxhounds, and Cloghan Castle Harriers, for Tipperary and King's County, are out almost every day, and seldom fail to afford keen enjoyment. The master and his friend and companion, Mr. T. Craddock, are horsemen of the first quality.'

These gentlemen were such terrific entertainers that eventually one of their soirees was reported in the social pages of the London Times. The English Police read this with great interest and soon after, Captain Wright and Mr. T. Craddock were arrested and returned to England. It seems they had both enjoyed a penchant for embezzling money from their former employer – a large bank!

Local legend had it that one died in prison while the other came back years later and was seen digging for something near the castle.

Chapter 15

20th Century - Tea Planters, Jute Planters and Soldiers

20th Century - Tea Planters, Jute Planters and Soldiers

Cloghan Castle was purchased from the Land Commission in 1908 by a tea planter from India, Major Durnford, and was rented to a Captain Arthur Burdett of Coolfin who was robbed of his shotguns during 'the troubles' of 1922.

Later, a retired jute planter from India, Colonel Wood, took over Cloghan Castle. His daughter, related through her maternal grandmother to the Eyres of Eyrecourt, descendants from Moores and Maddens, married an Irish Guards Officer called Major Patrick Whiteford and they ran a very successful market garden here until 1956. We used to enjoy stories from our dear friend Valerie Landon who grew up near here and was Pamela's close friend. We had the pleasure of meeting up with Pamela in London a few years ago.

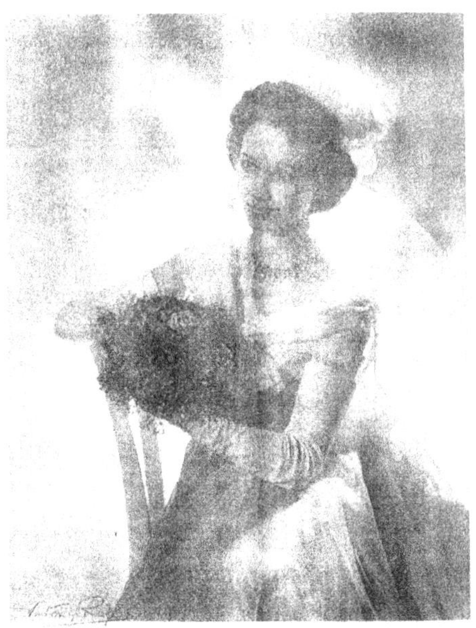

Pamela Wood upon her presentation to court

From 1956 until October 1972, Major Denis Bowes-Daly MC owned Cloghan Castle. He was the grandson of Lord Dunsandle, who owned 17,000 acres, and inherited one of the finest Georgian houses in Ireland – Dunsandle House, Athenry, County Galway, together with a vast landholding. He himself told me that this land was in his family for 1,600 years! Bowes-Daly went to Eton College and the Royal Military Academy at Sandhurst. He was an officer in the Royal Horse Guards 1918-1927, A. D. C. to the Viceroy of India 1923-1926, Master of the Galway Blazers 1928-1930 and later Joint Master. He was born in 1900 and married Diana Lascelles in 1927.

During the 1939-1945 war, he was awarded the Military Cross for an outstanding act of bravery. By 1950 he was divorced and re-married to Melosine, the twice-divorced previous Joint Master of the Galway Blazers. Major Bowes-Daly MC was a handsome man who would be described as a "gentleman of the old school". What happened to him beggars description:-

The title went elsewhere due to a legal dispute. He himself told me that his grandparent's marriage had been declared legally invalid. In 1947, the Galway Blazers were involved in a colossal row with the then Bishop of Galway over the presence of Major Bowes-Daly's soon-to-be second wife. An excerpt from a 1986 review in the RTE Guide describes the furore at the heart of the Irish Catholic church:-

> *"Because she had divorced and remarried in England, she found herself at the centre of an unmerciful clerical row, and was denounced by three western Bishops. Their main bone of contention was that 'a woman who had remarried should not be given a position of public honour"* i.e. the Mastership of the Galway Blazers.

In a statement published on December 27th 1947, the Archbishop of Tuam – Dr Walsh, the Bishop of Galway – Dr Browne, and the Bishop of Clonfert – Dr Digan, said, *"We feel that opposition to the hunt is justified. Catholic people do not refuse ordinarily civil rights and courtesies to people who remarry, but they do object to the demand that they should show public honour to those who do."*

An Irish solution was found. The Government Land Commission decided to eject them from Dunsandle so, as Major Bowes-Daly told me, he demolished it himself. I had been told by others that it was demolished after he left. I quote him, "Nobody but a Daly will ever live there!" The compensation (what little there was) went eventually towards the purchase of Cloghan Castle and a ranch in Tanganyika, from which he was later ejected at 48 hours notice by President Nyerere.

Mrs Melosine Daly was born in Galway, the daughter of a British Army General from an aristocratic Anglo-Irish family. They were a tough, brave and uncompromising tribe and many of that ilk were arrogant beyond belief. An interview with Melosine 'Melon' from Ann Morrow's *Picnic in a Foreign Land* describes her indomitable spirit. She also describes in more detail how, during the handover to the Irish Free State in 1922, her mother's car was ambushed and her throat cut, but due to being place upside down in the car boot on the way to hospital, she survived! Her daughter Melosine was a very strong character who attracted great affection from some. I have to confess however that when we met, it was instant mutual dislike on both sides.

When the Daly's were in Africa, Cloghan Castle lay empty. In 1957, Father John Fahy, Parish Priest of Lusmagh, founded an organisation called Lia Fail. This was dedicated to land reform and a lot more besides. I would recommend anybody really interested in an extraordinary story to read Chapter 5 of the book, *Offaly History and Society,* published by Geographical Publications.

Lusmagh had a population of 3,643 in 1841, 2,184 in 1851 and 554 in 1911. In 1965, the population was only 492. The Protestant population in the Republic of Ireland had collapsed since 1922 due to emigration, land redistribution, fear, intermarriage and a certain amount of "ethnic cleansing". Many churches, which had once held full congregations, now held services for less than a dozen. Power had passed to the Roman Catholic Bishops and by the 1950s, they were more powerful than the government. To cross swords with the Archbishop of Dublin was to invite extinction. High hopes for the new Irish State had not then materialised largely due to the world recession and the economic blockade of Irish products to Britain, brought in by the ill-advised action of Eamonn DeValera over Land Annuities. Better days were yet to come.

Father John Fahy was chaplain to the IRA in Scotland in 1919-1920 when he was linked with Dundee's Leading Communist, Bob Stewart. In 1929, he instigated a land annuities campaign in East Galway, and had been prosecuted by the Government in 1931 when he was trying to buy machine guns for the IRA to overthrow the Free State. The Garda at that time believed him to be one of the most active IRA organisers in East Galway. It is thought that on pressure from his Bishop, he gave up these pursuits until the founding of Lia Fail in 1957.

Basically, the intention was to create a paradise where all foreigners and Protestants were expelled from Ireland, the land redistributed into smallholdings, the border removed, and DeValera and his ministers hanged.

The Daly's were described as foreigners (South African) and when, during the early activities against foreigners, some of the participants ended up in Banagher jail, these 'rebels' were released by fellow parishioners to hide in Cloghan Castle where they did considerable damage, for which the Daly's as ratepayers had to pay a proportion.

The row that followed involved the government at its highest level, the bishops, the Gardai and led to jail for some. It also led to the loss of jobs and the resignation of Father Fahy.

If I had known one-tenth of this history in 1972, nothing on earth would have induced me to purchase Cloghan Castle. I later got to know some of the 'rebels' and their descendants very well indeed. Some have not changed any of the earlier revolutionary zeal, but others are the mildest least revolutionary types I have ever known. The children of most of them have done very well in life and are part of the new elite with good degrees and good salaries.

One descendant was a recent tour guide at the Castle, and I handed him the Offaly book and told him to read Chapter 5. When I had done so, he and his fellow guides collapsed laughing with a mixture of pride and ridicule. "Why?" I asked "did they do it?" "Because Father Fahy said to do it and his word was law". I have had the same reply from others involved more closely.

I liked Major Bowes Daly very much and felt sorry for him. He was born into a sector of society in terminal decline, which was accelerated by the outrage of the Bishops. When the Daly's returned to Ireland, they tried various enterprises, without success, and it was during this era that the front of the Georgian section was concreted, parts of the estate sold off, and the Virginia Creeper which covered the whole back of the castle, cut down. Eventually, losses at Lloyds of London led to the sale of Cloghan in 1972.

The horrific mail bombing in July 1982 of horses and Cavalrymen near Hyde Park Barracks in London by the IRA, killed Major Daly's beloved grandson – a tragedy from which he, aged in his 80s, never recovered. Many years later, Elyse and I had a delightful afternoon with his thoughtful son, Lt Col Denis Daly. We sat over lunch in the walled garden and enjoyed hearing pleasant memories of spending his school holidays in Cloghan with his stepmother and father.

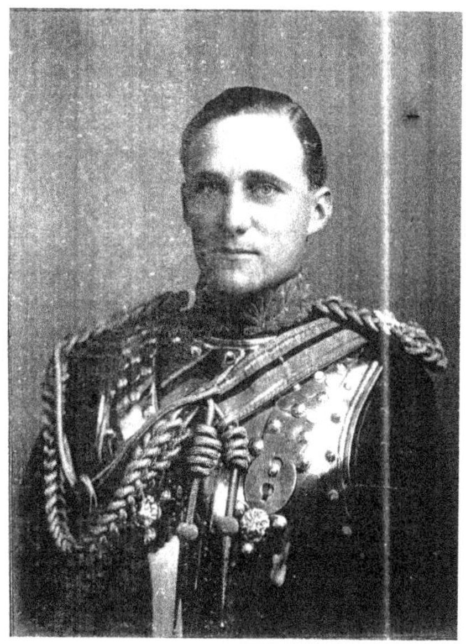

Major Denis Bowes-Daly

Chapter 16

Sic Transit Gloria Mundi

Sic Transit Gloria Mundi

Up to now we have had on this land two Irish Saints, a Norman Sinner (William de Burgo), Irish Chieftains and a Norman family of Moores who became very Irish indeed. We have had the Anglo-Irish Graves, Durnfords and Woods and an Irish family of Dalys who reached the top echelons of society in England.

I am none of these, being born in Colonial New Zealand of Irish parents. With the exception of one English great-great-grandfather (whose ancestors were thought to have come from Scotland), my family tree is a mixture of Scottish and ancient Irish. I'm a Donovan Thompson and the Thompsons were shipping merchants who moved their headquarters from Ayr to the newly built city of Derry in 1614. They were in all three sieges in the 17th century and were Presbyterians. I was brought up, on my arrival from New Zealand on my 7th birthday, in the old family home overlooking the city, which had housed six generations of us.

On the Donovan side, I am descended from a younger son of Colonel The O'Donovan (the clan chief) in 1690. He fought with his brothers in their own regiment (1,200 men) on the losing side of the Jacobite Wars, and the authentic family tree goes back to the year 230 AD, all in Ireland. I was brought up in Derry, Donegal and Down with a grounding in all three non-English traditions in Ireland. I also lived in England for 25 years.

In my lifetime, I have seen this country go from backwardness and poverty to a fully-fledged forward-moving European State. I believe that when and if the Northern hatreds have been resolved, this country will shed the overbearing tragedies of its past and move on to a great future.

The history of Cloghan Castle is in many ways a smaller edition of the history of Ireland. The castle or its owners were involved in many landmark events and these reflect the mixture, which we all are. Cloghan was once a vast estate bordering the estates of Lord Rosse to the East and Lord Clanrickarde to the west. It is now a quaint old home set in lovely parkland in a mere 157 acres, surrounded by prosperous farms and many fine modern houses. It once represented most of the wealth in Lusmagh, but today is only a very small fraction of that total wealth. We do not require an imperial army to protect us, and we invite visitors to see and enjoy the castle. We are no longer part of an elite ruling minority – we are a tourist attraction.

In July 1991, a Minister of State officially opened the Castle to the public. There were about 80 people invited to the ceremony including many friends and neighbours. Refreshments were provided in the Main Guard and I went in to chat with members of the Kelly family sitting by the fireplace. Mr Paddy Kelly was by now a great age. He had once been the gamekeeper for the estate and also Commander of the Lusmagh IRA in 1922.

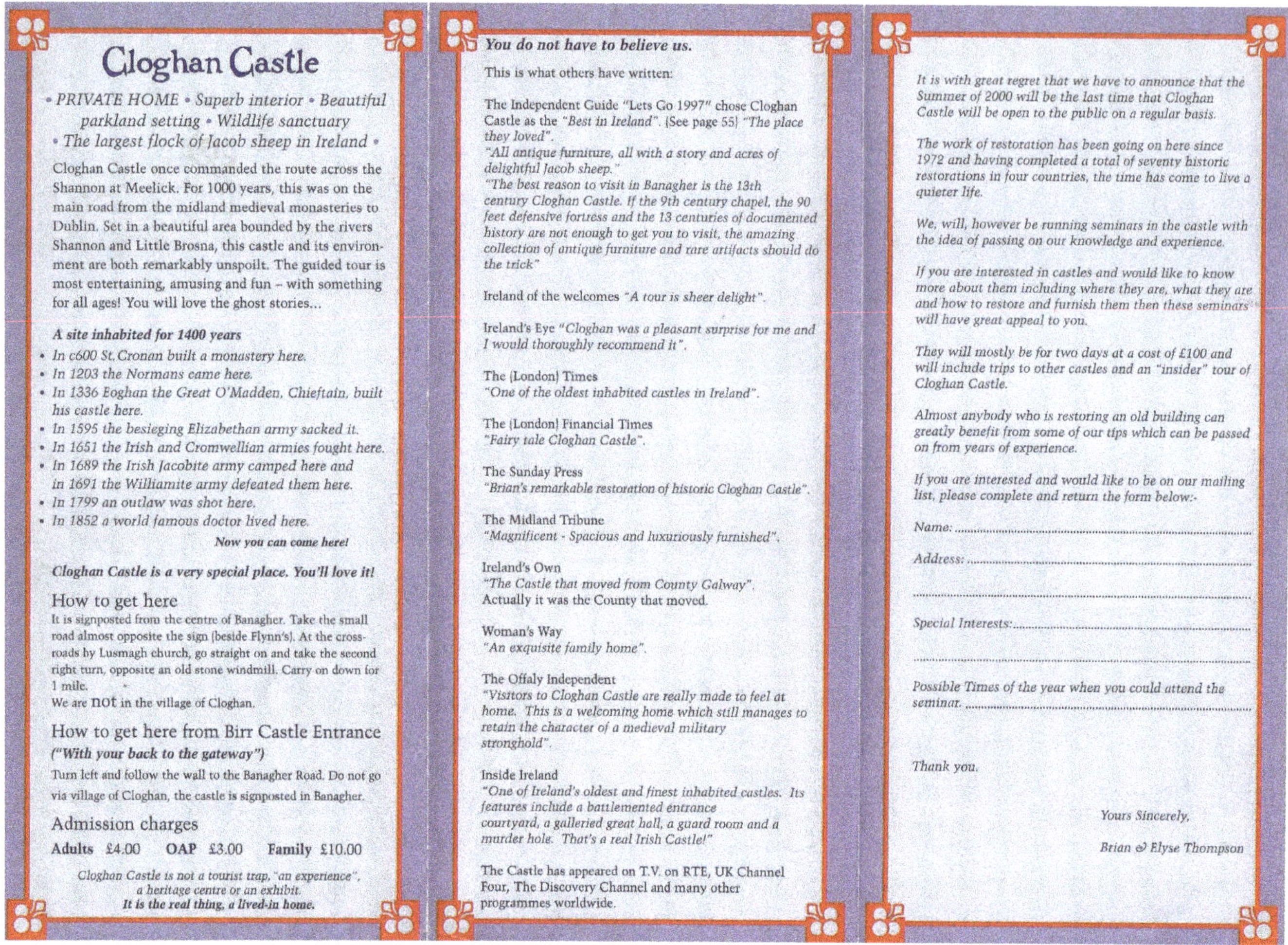

Cloghan Castle

• *PRIVATE HOME* • *Superb interior* • *Beautiful parkland setting* • *Wildlife sanctuary* • *The largest flock of Jacob sheep in Ireland* •

Cloghan Castle once commanded the route across the Shannon at Meelick. For 1000 years, this was on the main road from the midland medieval monasteries to Dublin. Set in a beautiful area bounded by the rivers Shannon and Little Brosna, this castle and its environment are both remarkably unspoilt. The guided tour is most entertaining, amusing and fun – with something for all ages! You will love the ghost stories...

A site inhabited for 1400 years

- *In c600 St. Cronan built a monastery here.*
- *In 1203 the Normans came here.*
- *In 1336 Eoghan the Great O'Madden, Chieftain, built his castle here.*
- *In 1595 the besieging Elizabethan army sacked it.*
- *In 1651 the Irish and Cromwellian armies fought here.*
- *In 1689 the Irish Jacobite army camped here and in 1691 the Williamite army defeated them here.*
- *In 1799 an outlaw was shot here.*
- *In 1852 a world famous doctor lived here.*

Now you can come here!

Cloghan Castle is a very special place. You'll love it!

How to get here

It is signposted from the centre of Banagher. Take the small road almost opposite the sign (beside Flynn's). At the crossroads by Lusmagh church, go straight on and take the second right turn, opposite an old stone windmill. Carry on down for 1 mile.

We are not in the village of Cloghan.

How to get here from Birr Castle Entrance

("With your back to the gateway")

Turn left and follow the wall to the Banagher Road. Do not go via village of Cloghan, the castle is signposted in Banagher.

Admission charges

Adults £4.00 **OAP** £3.00 **Family** £10.00

Cloghan Castle is not a tourist trap, "an experience", a heritage centre or an exhibit.
It is the real thing, a lived-in home.

You do not have to believe us.

This is what others have written:

The Independent Guide "Lets Go 1997" chose Cloghan Castle as the "*Best in Ireland*". (See page 55) "*The place they loved*".
"*All antique furniture, all with a story and acres of delightful Jacob sheep.*"
"*The best reason to visit in Banagher is the 13th century Cloghan Castle. If the 9th century chapel, the 90 feet defensive fortress and the 13 centuries of documented history are not enough to get you to visit, the amazing collection of antique furniture and rare artifacts should do the trick*"

Ireland of the welcomes "*A tour is sheer delight*".

Ireland's Eye "*Cloghan was a pleasant surprise for me and I would thoroughly recommend it*".

The (London) Times
"*One of the oldest inhabited castles in Ireland*".

The (London) Financial Times
"*Fairy tale Cloghan Castle*".

The Sunday Press
"*Brian's remarkable restoration of historic Cloghan Castle*".

The Midland Tribune
"*Magnificent - Spacious and luxuriously furnished*".

Ireland's Own
"*The Castle that moved from County Galway*".
Actually it was the County that moved.

Woman's Way
"*An exquisite family home*".

The Offaly Independent
"*Visitors to Cloghan Castle are really made to feel at home. This is a welcoming home which still manages to retain the character of a medieval military stronghold*".

Inside Ireland
"*One of Ireland's oldest and finest inhabited castles. Its features include a battlemented entrance courtyard, a galleried great hall, a guard room and a murder hole. That's a real Irish Castle!*"

The Castle has appeared on T.V. on RTE, UK Channel Four, The Discovery Channel and many other programmes worldwide.

It is with great regret that we have to announce that the Summer of 2000 will be the last time that Cloghan Castle will be open to the public on a regular basis.

The work of restoration has been going on here since 1972 and having completed a total of seventy historic restorations in four countries, the time has come to live a quieter life.

We, will, however be running seminars in the castle with the idea of passing on our knowledge and experience.

If you are interested in castles and would like to know more about them including where they are, what they are and how to restore and furnish them then these seminars will have great appeal to you.

They will mostly be for two days at a cost of £100 and will include trips to other castles and an "insider" tour of Cloghan Castle.

Almost anybody who is restoring an old building can greatly benefit from some of our tips which can be passed on from years of experience.

If you are interested and would like to be on our mailing list, please complete and return the form below:-

Name: ....

Address: ....

....

Special Interests: ....

....

Possible Times of the year when you could attend the seminar. ....

Thank you.

Yours Sincerely,

Brian & Elyse Thompson

One side of the tourism brochure about the castle (see page 144 for reverse)

Our dearest friend, Valerie Landon, joined us all. A gentle soul, witty yet kind, and not a little eccentric, Valerie had grown up friends with Pamela Wood of Cloghan Castle. Valerie's father had been prominent in the locale as an Anglo-Irish Captain during World War I. Valerie was also a humble person, so we discovered from others that, during World War II, as a young woman, she was self sacrificially courageous as evidenced by the fact she had been "Mentioned in Dispatches" (twice!). Finally, she was a talented ceramicist and ran Crannog Pottery in Banagher. Anyway, Valerie and Paddy were sitting by the fireplace with their cups of tea. Elyse was walking past with another tray of cakes, when she heard Valerie ask of Paddy, *"Tell me, why Did they Never shoot Daddy?"* Elyse managed to not drop her tray! Paddy's response was, "Well…I always liked the Captain."

A little while later, Paddy took me aside, and said, "I am so very glad, that I would NOT let them burn the Castle." When he died, I flew our flag from the battlements at half-mast for two weeks as a mark of considerable respect and gratitude.

Observations

Because I've had thousands of tenants over the years, both in England and in the United States, it may seem that I am sympathetic to the old order.

Nothing could be further from the truth.

Renting property to people looking for a short term home is one thing but renting land which requires complete dedication from year to year is quite a different matter.

Despite what the history books, prepared on the views of the side that won, tell us, it is surely obvious that many landlords were very good and town after town in Ireland has shops and business premises erected by landlords which are quite splendid.

In Wales, farms were rented on an annual basis with horrendous consequences. In Northern Ireland, there was 'Tenant right' which gave the tenants some kind of tenure and compensation for improvements. In Scotland, the Clan Chiefs, who were in many cases related to their tenants, engaged in wholesale evictions to make way for sheep. The denuded Highlands are their lasting memorial.

During a recent tour of Cloghan Castle, some Hungarians told me their history and devastation from the potato famine not to mention centuries of Ottoman rule which made Irish sufferings look like good times.

I read that after the famine Ireland had a 'boom' and that before independence Ireland was the seventh most prosperous nation in the world. I have also read that recent DNA testing has proved that the native indigenous population of the British Isles, English, Scottish, Irish and Welsh all share the same DNA base which rather shatters the myths of Anglo Saxon superiority and myths of our Celtic separateness.

In my opinion, the medieval systems of land-owning stemming from the king downwards to create a nightmare of land held by tenants and sub-tenants created a social system which was the opposite of freedom.

There are very few descendants of the Anglo Irish aristocracy around today but I know of many wealthy families who owe their wealth to ancestors who were 'rack renters' making a fortune from the sufferings of the very poor.

Many of the old landlords rented substantial farms to Irish Catholics who subsequently subdivided their land at extortionate rates to landless families. I also know of many Protestants who were burned out of their homes so that their land could be subdivided to those hungry for extra land and a good many of these were ordinary hard-working farmers themselves who just happened to be Protestant.

The system was pernicious. The separation of people because of their religion was awful, but I am not convinced that all our troubles were the fault of the 'wicked English'. At the time of the famine, many landlords were purchasers or descendants of purchasers of their lands, as distinct from those whose holdings derived from Elizabethan, Cromwellian and Williamite confiscations.

Chapter 17

The Retainers

The Retainers

The history of Cloghan Castle has hitherto dealt with the owners and their descendants, but what of those who cared for them?

Men and women who devoted a large part of their lives to the Castle and its estate and who in many ways actually gave up their lives defending it. They too loved the place and I for one believe that some of them are still here.

Ghostly figures have been seen and heard by many people and I suppose that in due course I shall join them. Their descendants have often fared better in life than the descendants of those who were their employers. A lot of our tour guides, themselves descendants of former tenants and employees, have gone on to obtain excellent degrees and salaries, which are a constant source of wonder and pride.

Nearly 150 years ago, a one-armed veteran of the Crimean War came here to run the farm for Mr Graves. A short time ago, I was about to cross the road in Birr, when the owner of a brand new top of the range car waved to me as he passed by. It was a direct descendant of the old soldier. This descendant is highly intelligent and soon became one of the most successful entrepreneurs in all of Ireland. Time and time again, we get visits from people whose ancestors lived and worked here in the past. They all speak lovingly of the happy times their forebears had here. Times have changed, and a staff outing which would have produced a sizeable crowd 100 years ago, would today consist of my wife and myself!

Soldiers would have constantly patrolled the battlements, a priest would have been in attendance, a gatekeeper would always be on duty, and countless servants would have kept the wood and turf fires burning in ancient times. In Victorian and Georgian times, the cook and her helpers would have supplied excellent meals for the family and guests. The grooms would have looked after the Hunters and the hounds and the gamekeeper tried to protect the game from poachers. Governesses and nannies would have tended the children and watchful policemen would have lived on the estate to protect the owners.

We have had descendants of the family coachmen here to stay from America, whilst the descendants of a late coachman own a number of neighbouring farms. When the castle owners were away in Dublin, Mayo or England, the staff had the place to themselves and it became home for them and not just a place of work. Their thoughts and dreams became just as valid a part of the inner fabric of this castle as the hopes of their employers.

I have started to plant ornamental trees around the Castle in memory of members of my own family and we will plant trees in memory of the others who lived and worked here.

In 1996, we had an experience in connection with the daughter of a former employee and I wrote the story for the local newspaper as follows:

Going Home – If It Can Be Found

Mrs Bridget Candlin died in England on 8th February 1996. She was born in Ireland in 1911 and her birth was registered in Birr on 5th February 1912. She was the daughter of a carpenter, Edward McGee and her mother, Frances, was formerly a Murray from Lusmagh. She spent the first years of her life very happily in the house where she was born, but at the age of eight was taken away and put, with her sister, in an orphanage in England. One can only speculate how dreadful that was as she always said that the first years of her life were the happiest and she would like to be buried where she was born. Two weeks ago, Brian Thompson was astounded to get a telephone call from the owner of Kinnity Castle – "Brian, I have a guest here with a most unusual request to make of you." The request was certainly unusual – the man wished to bury his mother-in-law in the grounds of Cloghan Castle!

It turned out that the good lady in question had been cremated and her two daughters and son-in-law had spent nearly two weeks trying to find Cloghan Castle for that was where she was born and that is where she had wanted to be buried. They telephoned Bord Failte who had never heard of Cloghan Castle and they got the same answer from Offaly Tourism, and a host of other organisations, including Dooly's Hotel in Birr. One lady who ran a B&B in the village of Cloghan thought that Cloghan Castle was a youth hostel but did not know where it was.

It was bad enough for the Thompsons to be faced with the possibility of a burial at their home, but to learn that 30,000 leaflets issued annually and a great deal of expensive advertising had evidently not put Cloghan Castle on the tourist map even in Offaly, was a bit too much. Brian and Elyse Thompson thought about the situation before them and decided that those born in a place were of that place, and Bridget deserved to come home. She was duly placed in the Castle Chapel in a very small wooden box where she stayed for a week.

The Thompsons put her daughters in touch with Mrs Margaret Barton who with Mr Dinny Kelly, is the local historian, and her distant relatives were duly located. Unprepared to put poor Bridget in an unmarked piece of land, they thought of an idea which delighted her daughters. A tree planted in a splendid position facing the castle was planted in her honour and she was placed beneath it. The local Parish Priest, Father Patrick Geoghan, very kindly agreed to conduct the ceremony and on Wednesday, 13th March 1996 at three o'clock in the afternoon, amidst snow and rain, Mrs Bridget Candlin was duly laid to rest in the company of her many relatives. The very cold party then retired to Cloghan Castle for afternoon tea before a huge log fire. Bridget is now back home where her tree will look at the childhood home she loved so much. The Thompsons are now trying to figure out how to let Offaly Tourism know that Cloghan Castle exists!"

When the O'Madden climbed his horse to go to war, his retainers went with him. The Moores had employees of every variety. Soldiers guarded the place in Cromwellian and Jacobite times, and coins fell from their ragged clothing to be pulled up centuries later.

In past eras of hunting, shooting and fishing the experts in their field tried hard to make the owners and their guests look good, even when they were quite obviously not! Like many rural householders in Ireland, the Retainers would have been thought of, and treated, as 'family', *and in some cases...actually were.*

The Story of John Pearson – Whose Mother was Thought to have been a Nurse at Cloghan Castle

I am greatly indebted to Mr and Mrs Henry Pollard who are historians for the Claremont School for the Deaf, in Dublin, for the following excerpt from "*The Journal of the British Deaf History Society* published in December 2001.

The First British Deaf Juror

In the past eight years debates on the communication support for the Deaf in the British courtroom and, in particular on the issue of Deaf jurors, have been controversial and generated great interest within the Deaf community in the present day. There was a 1994 case of a would-be deaf juror who was dismissed from jury service on grounds of a ruling under a section of the 1974 Juries Act. This ruling stated that any person is ineligible for jury service if the person has a "physical disability or insufficient understanding of English." Newspaper headlines screamed, "Britain's first deaf juror denied 'basic human rights'!" The term, 'Britain's first deaf juror', raises an interesting question. There were some deaf jurors in the past and the very first case we came across was that of a deaf and dumb juror from Ireland in 1843. Perhaps the following account may be of interest to campaigners battling for the Deaf's right to be selected as jurors in the law-courts.

The information was first noted in the 28th Annual Report of the National Institution for the Education of Deaf and Dumb children of the poor, Claremont, near Dublin issued in 1844, which reported an account of an inquest taken from an undated and unnamed provincial newspaper. After a long search, it was confirmed reported in The Leinster Express, 16 December 1843, on page 3, column1. Some research work was carried out with reference to details in the report shown below and they are indicated by the numbered references.

Inquest – A Deaf and Dumb Juror!

On Friday morning last,[1] *a small farmer named William Larkin, residing at Inchanalee*[2] *in the parish of Lusmagh, sent his son, a lad aged about twelve years, to the forge of a smith named Quirk,*[3] *on business. About half an hour after his arrival there, he fell down on the ground, gave three screams, moved for a few minutes as if in a fit and then expired. The deceased was apparently in good health at the time, and was not known to have been subject to any kind of fits.*

On Saturday an inquest was held on the body, before James Dillon, Esq.,[4] *coroner, when, after a patient investigation, the jury found that the deceased 'died by the visitation of God'. A circumstance of more than ordinary interest was connected with this inquest, which may not be deemed unworthy of public notoriety, and will show in some measure the utility of Claremont Institution – which combines in itself everything that excites sympathy or draws forth charity, and it is hoped a deeper interest will be felt in the Institution for the Deaf and Dumb Poor of Ireland. When the coroner arrived at that part of Lusmagh, where the body lay, which is very thinly inhabited, to hold the inquest, he found the police authorities*[5] *there laboriously endeavouring to collect the minimum number required by law*[6] *to constitute a coroner's jury. After an unusual delay, he saw amongst those assembled an intelligent-looking young man, whose name was previously withheld from him, when he required to know the cause from those around him who informed him of that person's incompetence, as he was both deaf and dumb.*

The coroner then beckoned the young man to approach him. He immediately complied; then the coroner wrote down on a slip of paper, 'Can you either read or write?' the young man took up a pen, and in a very fine, legible, and commanding hand, replied, 'Yes; both.'

Coroner: *What is your name?*

Young man: *John Pearson*

Coroner: *Then I am about to swear you on this inquest, to assist me in investigating the cause of death.*

Pearson: *I know nothing of the death, as I was not up at the forge when the young man died.*

Coroner: *It is not as a witness, but as a juror, I mean to attest you; do you understand me?*

Pearson: *Yes, sir, perfectly well.*

The coroner then wrote for him the following form of obligation, pending the writing of which Pearson paid very marked attention:- 'You, John Pearson, shall well and diligently inquire when, how, and by what means Patrick Larkin, of whose body you shall have the view, came by his death. So help you God.'

Pearson then took off his hat, raised the Gospels in his right hand, surveyed the obligation attentively, looked up to heaven in a reverential manner, kissed the book, and quietly repaired to view the body. On his return, he took up his position in the rere[7] *of the coroner, anxiously watching the progress of the proceedings, as taken down by that gentleman from the testimony of the witnesses, and, at the close of each, he put the individual through a strict and searching cross-examination. When the verdict was about to be recorded, he took up the finding, as noted by the coroner from the evidence, compared it with the minutes, and wherever either legal or medical technical phrases appeared, he required to be informed of their simple meaning, or to what they had reference; after which, when satisfied, he wrote his name at the foot thereof.*

On inquiry, we find that Pearson's parents[8] *originally held some responsible situation under the O'Moores of Cloghan Castle*[9]*, where they acquired means to enable them to put him into the Claremont Institution, where he was liberally educated*[10], *and ultimately bound as an apprentice to a cabinet-maker of notoriety in Dublin, and he is now a tradesman of no mean pretensions."*

For Deaf history records, John Pearson was probably the first British Deaf juror and the year was 1843.

In 1994, Mrs Elaine Heath of Denver, Norfolk, the would-be deaf juror, was dismissed from jury service because Judge John Binns was not convinced that she would be able to follow the proceedings. Whilst in court, Mrs Heath had the use of Palantype so that she could read what was said in the court. Surely the presence of today's new technology and the positive views of Lord Irvine, the Lord Chancellor, who said, in June 2001, that it was important to ensure "that the lay bench was as representative of the community it serves as possible" indicate that the ruling under the section of 1975 Juries Act needs to be revised. Interestingly, Lord Irvine would consider lifting the ban on deaf magistrates.

On the subject of the jury, oddly enough, the jury can sit through a long case without saying a word. The jury remains dumb. There may be other disabilities about the jury besides its dumbness – that is, can members of the jury read or write? In a court case, the judge is seen making notes, and the counsel is also seen doing the same thing as well as reading documents of evidence. But surprisingly, the jurors are allowed neither pens nor pencils nor paper.

Alfred Tennyson once said, "Theirs is not to reason why; theirs is to find a verdict." In other words, John Pearson the deaf and dumb juror and the other members of the jury did give their verdict on the cause of the death of Patrick Larkin.

Finally, Lord Ashley remarked in 1994 that "it is the judge who must decide who can serve as a juror. Some judges have very old-fashioned ideas and views about deaf people. This amendment requires the judge to presume capability." The example set by Mr James Dillon, the coroner from Clara, who in 1843 after a written dialogue with John Pearson accepted him to be one of the members of the jury was admirable indeed.

Chapter 18

Complete Tour of The Building in 2003 and Searching for "Sheela"

Complete Tour of The Building in 2003 and Searching for Sheela

Searching for "Sheela"

In 1990, a considerable amount of work was done on rebuilding the battlements, which as mentioned had been 'slighted' in 1595.

It was then that I began a great search for the Sheela-na-Gig, the ancient fertility carving that should have been there. I explained to my workmen the rather obscene nature of this female figure and what exactly to look out for. They tolerated me for about a week, when, one sunny day after lunch, I was informed that they had found what I had been looking for. I rushed out in a great state of excitement but could see nothing. One of them went very considerately to collect my binoculars and we all trooped round to the west wall with great solemnity, as I tried to locate our obscure female figure. By the time my binoculars had discovered the well-built centrefold from Penthouse Magazine, so conveniently stuck to the wall just under the battlements, I was alone.

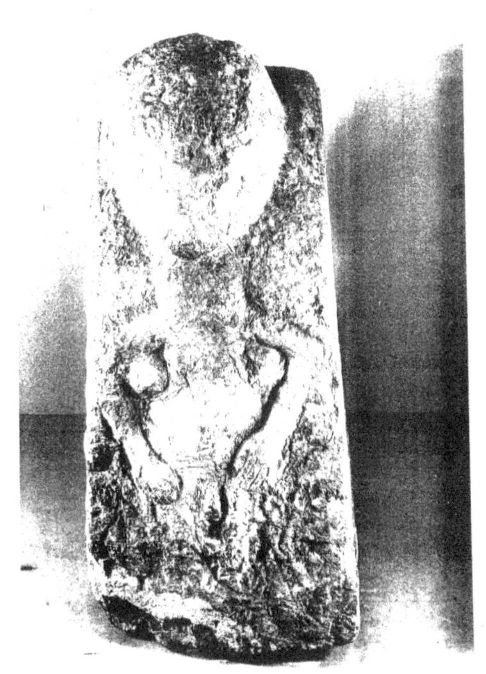

Sheela na Gig

I decided therefore to follow a more scholarly approach in future and discovered that Mr T L Cooke, who wrote *The Early History of Birr* in the 19th century, had purchased the Cloghan Castle Sheela. The Royal Society of Antiquaries of Ireland was most helpful and I was able to obtain from them an exact description of our Sheela together with the exact measurements of the stone.

I then went to the National Museum for further information, and as I walked into the building in Kildare Street, I found myself confronted with a whole plethora of Sheela's which had been removed from the basement where nobody in the past had been able to see such "disgusting sights". One of the Sheela's was said to come from somewhere 'near Birr'. The description fitted exactly that of the Cloghan Castle Sheela, and the stone was measured and found to be exactly that of the Cloghan Castle Sheela. The very worn head looked quite unlike the other carvings in the room and resembled to my eyes the head of a sheep. Cloghan-na-gCaora- the stone of the sheep.

The Building in 2003

I took over the castle in 1972. It had been lived in right up to that moment but was surrounded by ruined corrugated iron farm buildings, barely a recognisable cottage which had been used for pigs, derelict land which had to be completely cleared, overgrown gardens with sadly no remnants of the once plentiful orchards, and a castle in very poor condition indeed. We set to work on a project, which has cost many hundreds of thousands of pounds and which involved fifteen years of effort.

The Structure

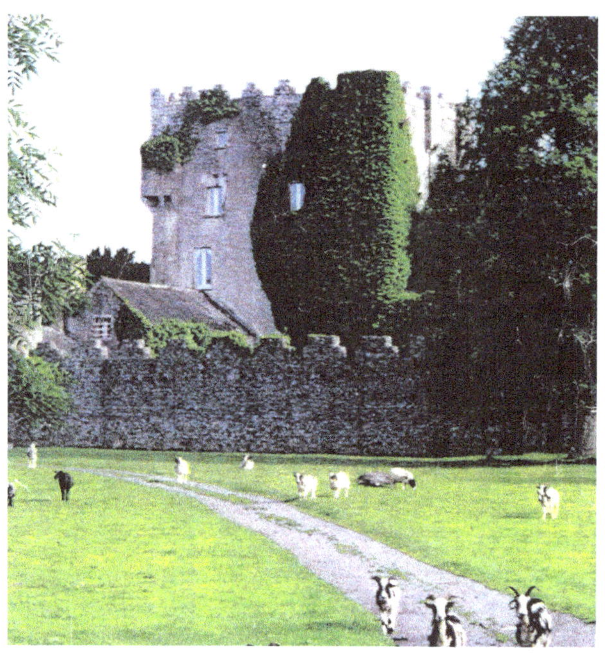

Elyse's Jacob sheep roaming around the castle grounds

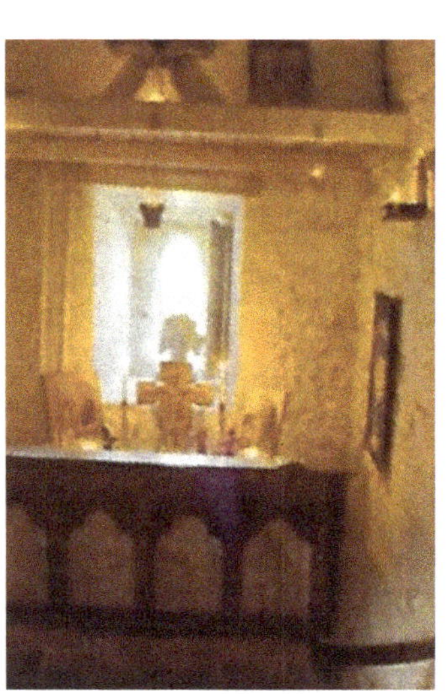

Chapel

The stone wall around the yew garden is thought to be 800 years old.

The keep was thought to have been built sometime after 1336 and before the year 1500 on much older foundations.

The sentry post is most unusual in size and shape and thought to be a small stone monk's cell from the original monastery. Incorporated within the castle walls, it is currently used as a little chapel and was so used during the occupancy of the Woods family and before.

The round towers in front of the castle are Cromwellian (c 1660) and the towers at the back are thought to be of the same age as the keep.

The kitchen wing at the back of the castle is thought to be Cromwellian in origin, but parts of it are much older than that.

The bawn wall on the eastern side of the castle is as old as the keep but the walls between the towers to the north and the south were rebuilt by Brian using old stones from estate walls. Work on them commenced in 1973 and took four men six years.

The battlements were blown off after the siege in 1595 and were rebuilt in 1983. 150 truckloads of stones had to be winched to the top of the keep.

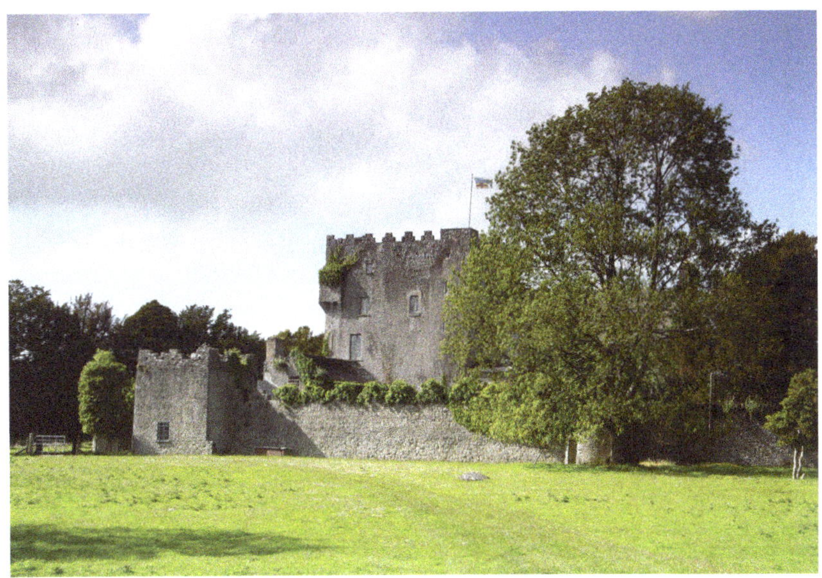

View of Cloghan castle

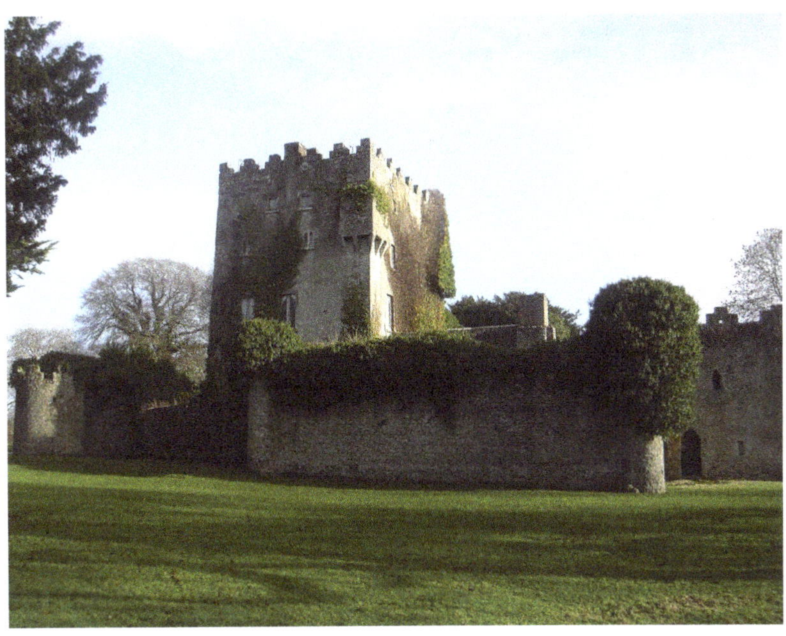

View of Cloghan castle from another angle

A Tour of the Castle in 2003 - The Contents have since been removed!

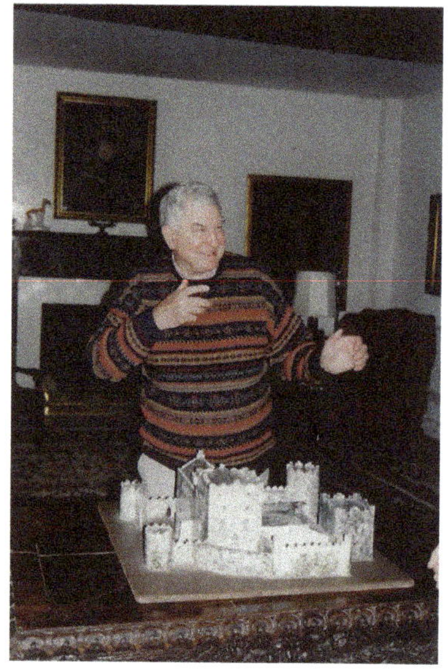

At the start of the tour with Brian

A striking feature of the castle at this time is the comfort and beauty of this ancient building which has been adapted for modern living without sacrificing any of its character.

The contents are a blend of many eras mixing ancient oak furniture and oil paintings with carpets from India and China, just as one would expect when a dwelling has been inhabited by the same family for many centuries. However in this case, the contents have not been in this building for that time but some of it has been in the Thompson family for many generations.

Oil fired central heating and modern bathrooms do not intrude into the character of the building, and they certainly make living a lot easier in an age without servants.

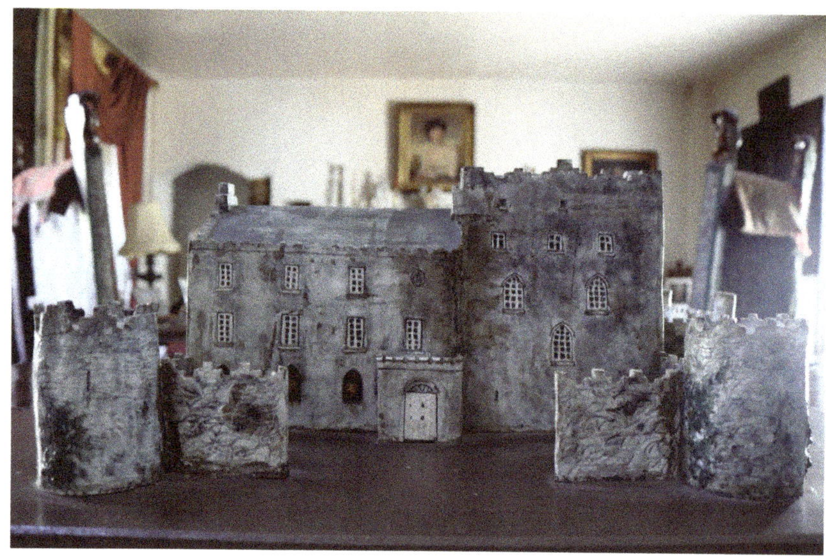

A Model of the Castle

One enters the castle by a small porch on the northern side of the building and steps down into the Great Hall which is some 51 feet long and two stories high with galleries at both ends.

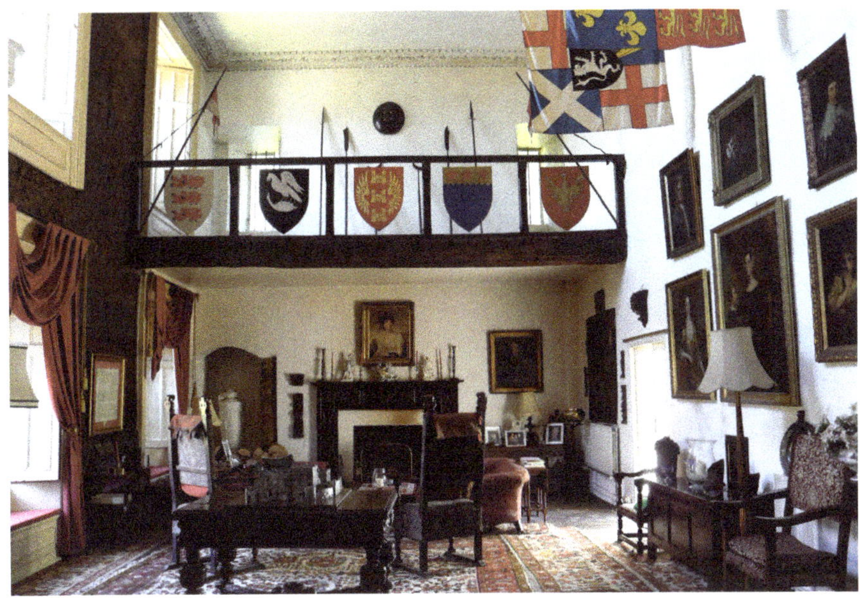

Great Hall

This is a striking room by any standards with armorial banners and shields of families connected with the castle in the past. The ancient elk horns (now in a museum) are thought to be 10,000 years old and there are four carved oak chests, one of them dated 1614. On and around the court cupboard are pikes, muskets, swords and bows to remind one of the castle's warlike past.

The oil paintings date from Elizabethan up to a mere 200 years old with oak panelling and carvings to complete the feeling of age.

The fine plaster ceiling was crafted around 200 years ago but was heavily damaged before 1972, so I had scaffolding erected and experts repaired it (at considerable expense).

The Great Hall was thought to have been created in two stages and the lower part of the room was probably an extension built by Cromwellians to house a garrison of soldiers. The top part, and the bedrooms above that, were erected by the Moore family in and around 1800 AD. The oak beam visible above the fireplace is around 350 years old.

When the Moores built their new extension, the upper part of what is now the Great Hall was a ballroom and they must have had some remarkable evenings there because by 1972 the floor was in very poor condition and had to be removed.

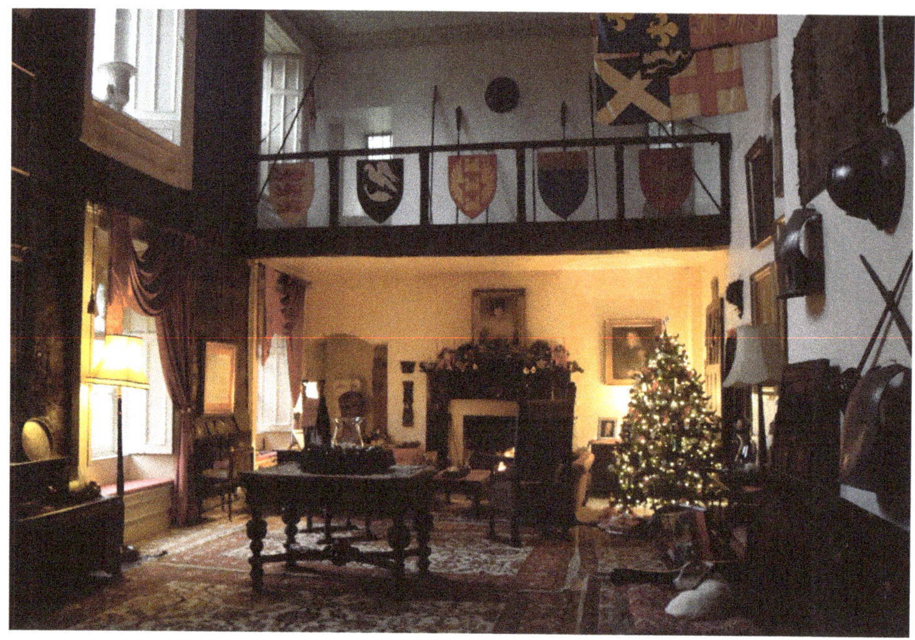

Great Hall at Christmas

The main staircase is made of wood and the beautiful yew bannister is probably 300 years old, grown here, carved here, and put in with love and care. Family portraits to the sides and Brian's maternal grandfather's grandfather clock some 200 years old from Ballynahinch County Down are features as one ascends to the library area.

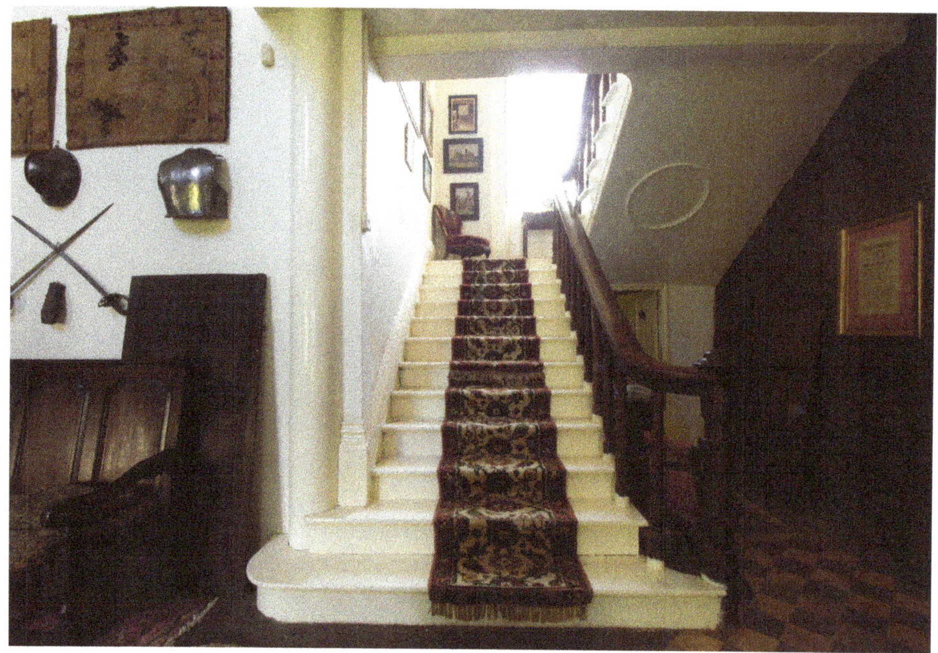

Main Staircase

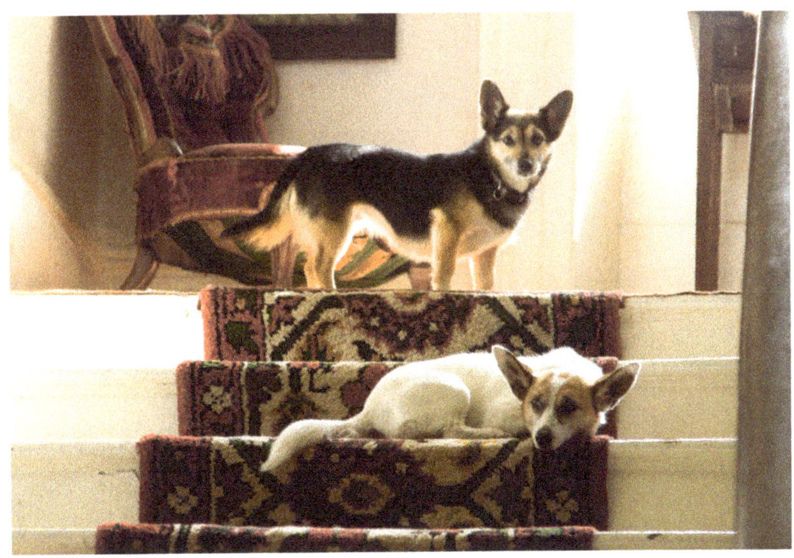

The dogs - strange looking rescues on the stairs

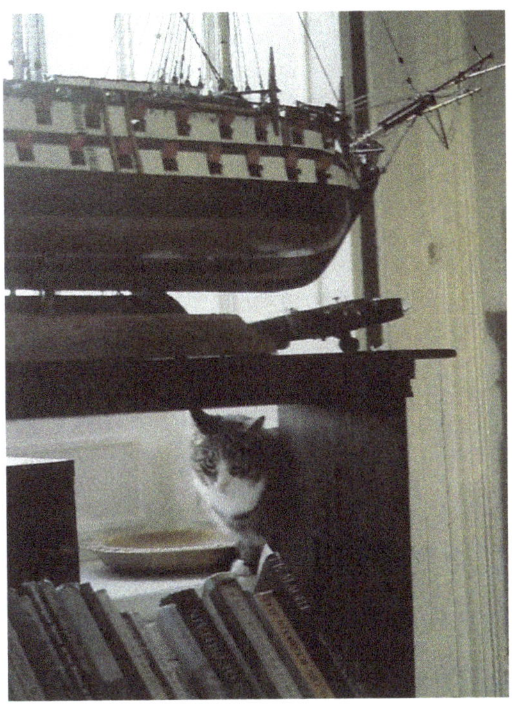

Bows seen next to model of the HMS Lion. With kind permission of Richard Surnam, Photographer & Author, *Castle Cats of Great Britain and Ireland*

Here is a remarkable collection of Victorian children's books and Brian's great grandfather's bookcase with his grandfather's books still in it. Brian's grandmother's grandfather was a naval officer during the Napoleonic wars and here is his cocked hat, telescope and other artefacts. There is a splendid model of HMS Lion the ship he sailed in as a midshipman in 1815.

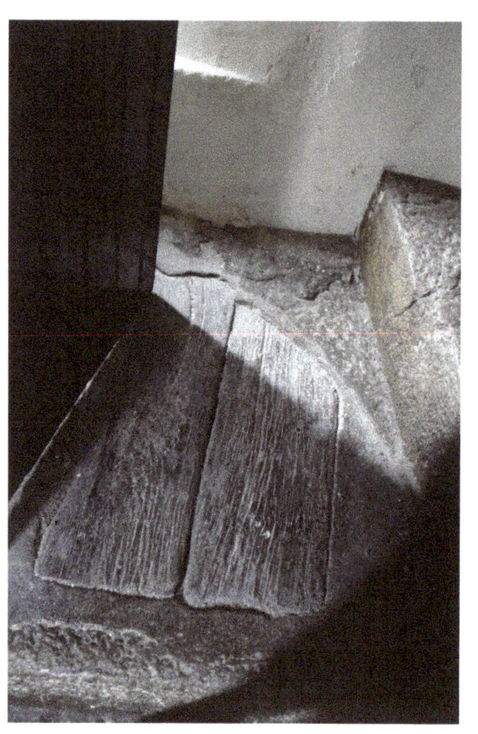

Murder Hole

A large window to the south looks out to a walled garden and beyond. A door here opens to a small area outside the Drawing Room and one is now within the ancient keep. A door to the left opens to the old stone staircase leading to the battlements. Beneath your feet is a metal plate which covers the "murder hole" used in times past to shoot down at those who have entered the castle by the old entrance and are trapped in a small hallway by the sentry post and main guard.

On the walls here are pictures of family members of previous castle owners including one of Captain-General Thomas Lee who sacked the place in 1595.

One now enters the Drawing Room which is clearly a very comfortable much-used room today. The TV set may be modern, but the chimney-piece beside it is 300 years old and the wooden panelling around the windows is 250 years old.

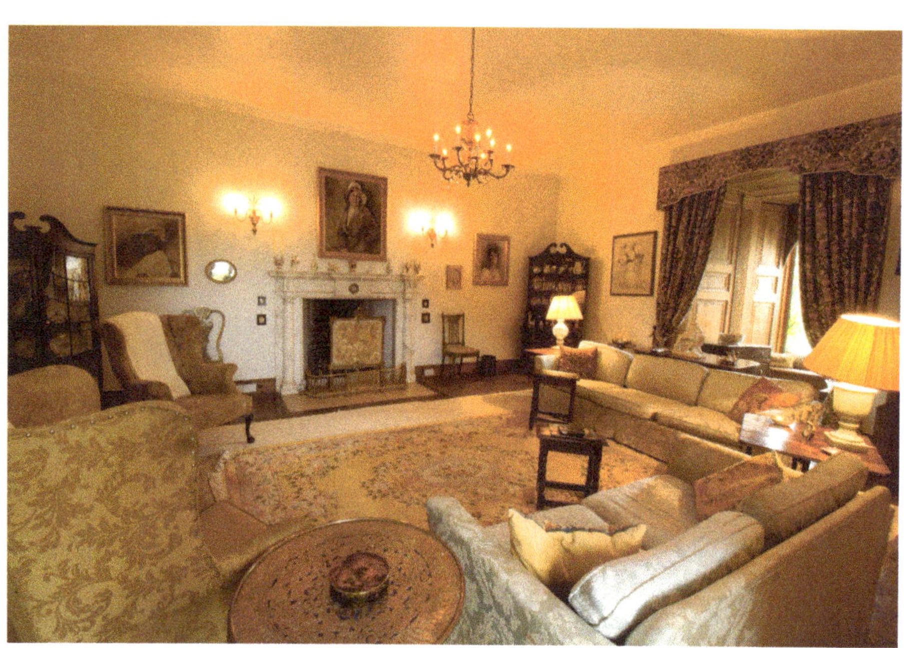

Drawing Room with kind permission from Tina Claffey

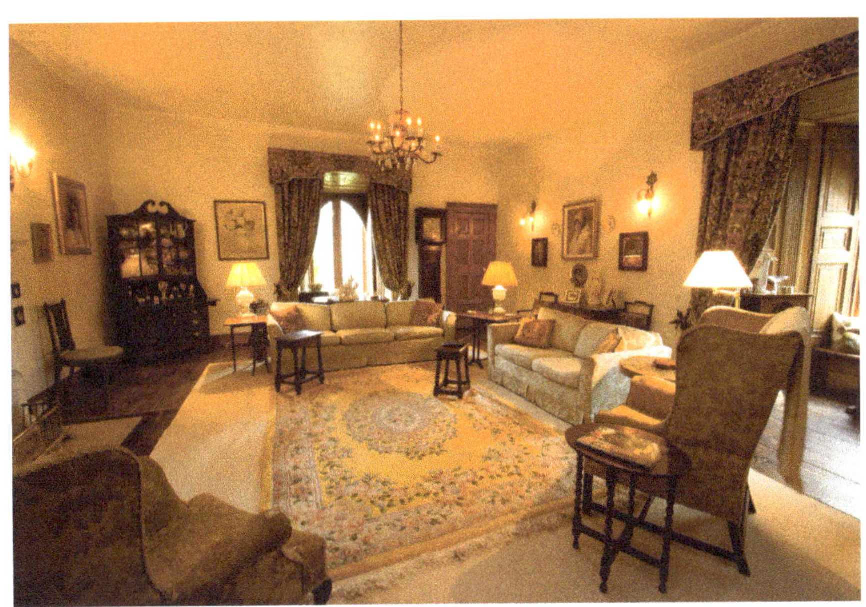

Drawing Room from another angle with kind permission from Tina Claffey

A wooden door at the far end of the room leads to a small closet with a slit window which probably once had a staircase leading to the floor above.

The Spode in a corner cupboard once belonged to the Duke of Sussex, the favourite son of King George III and just about everything in the room has a history, mostly in connection with the family here now. Close the wooden shutters, hide the TV, light the candles and one is back in time in a cosy warm atmosphere with surrounding walls up to 12 feet thick.

Up the stairs again past many family pictures to a small hallway and into the main bedroom which was described as the State Bedroom in the auction particulars of 1852.

Elyse Thompson is talented as an interior designer and it is not easy to mix contents of many eras into a building of great antiquity without destroying any of its original character. This, above all others, is her room and it is, without doubt, the most beautiful in the castle. (Photo on pg 147, sales particulars).

What was once a huge bleak room with a large fireplace, stone seated garderobe lavatory, and probably curtained four-poster bed is now a room of light and beauty. About two hundred years ago, the original room was subdivided so that the bedroom now has its own bathroom, dressing room and walk-in closet. A gold Chinese carpet and gold-tinged wallpaper ensure that sunlight from two large windows makes the whole room glow. A large tester bed with gold curtains complete the picture as do fine paintings and framed fans.

Crossing the hallway again one passes a small bathroom to the "Jacobean bedroom" so named because of the age of the ancient oak four-poster bed here. This part of the castle is a mere 200 years old but one would hardly believe this surrounded by such a collection of ancient oak furniture.

The next hallway looks out over the front park which is grazed by ornamental Jacob sheep. In the distance are surrounding trees, 80,000 of them. The old trees in the park are augmented by other ornamentals planted by the Thompsons for future inhabitants of the castle.

This narrow hallway is full of family memorabilia, pictures, sword and medals and leads to two other bedrooms.

The middle bedroom of the 200 years old wing has a delightful 200 years old four-poster bed and many toys, the oldest is a 200-year-old doll. The rare wool and silk pictures are of Irish scenes and the Davenport has been in the family for 150 years and still contains (in a hidden drawer) love letters written long before that by previous owners.

The end bedroom has windows looking over all the parkland to the front and rear of the castle and it contains a large tester bed which came originally from Guildhall Castle in Dromore, County Down. The bedside table and the Victorian chair beside it once belonged to Brian's great aunt for whom William Allingham wrote in 1849 the famous nursery rhyme, The Fairies, "Up the airy mountain, down the rushy glen, we dare not go a hunting for of little men".

Back down the corridor to the hall outside the State Bedroom and a door opens to the stone spiral stairway and we ascend it to the next floor. Here is a small bedroom with a four poster bed which is from Wales and is 300 years old. This little room was once the butler's pantry for the next room :

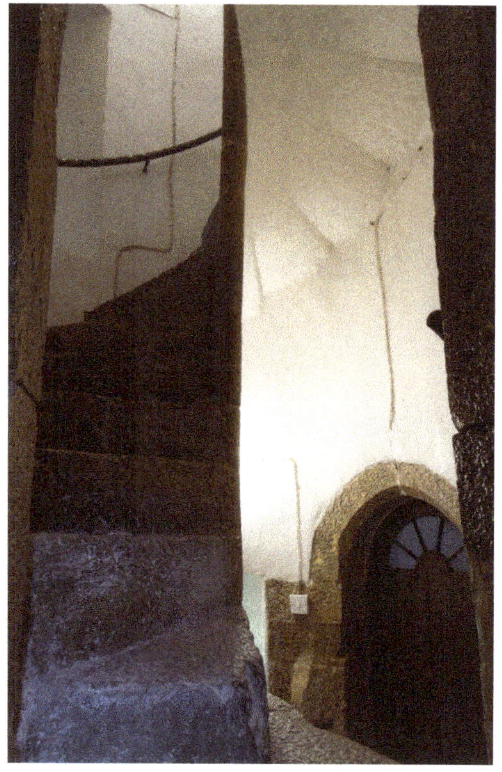

Spiral Staircase

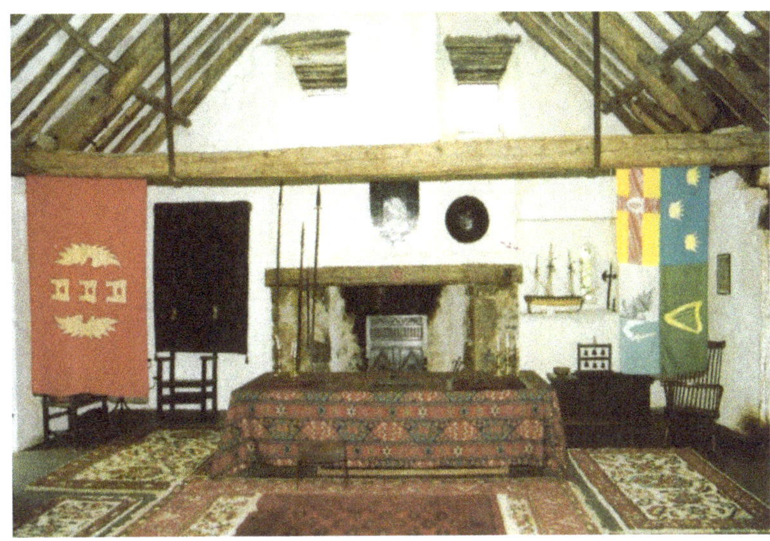

Court Room

The Court Room is two stories high and the roof timbers which are very dramatic were thought to have been put there four hundred years ago when the Moore family took over the burned out castle after the 1595 siege.

The huge fireplace was discovered behind a Victorian metal grate.

Used today merely for show, this remarkable room somehow still exudes the feeling of power it had when the Irish Clan Chiefs held court here.

In ancient times, the higher your rank, the higher up the castle you lived on the understandable basis that the Clan Chief had to be in the safest place.

One must remember that the configuration and use of rooms have changed over the centuries and that after 1595, the castle lost half a storey and number of "attic" rooms. This leads to some confusion amongst historical "experts" who have tried to date the building based on the shape of the battlements and their additions. After the top was blown off, the place was not reassembled exactly as it had been before and the castle was involved in at least four battles.

The Court Room, as it is now, is very rare in Ireland. Its preservation is due to the fact that the castle has been lived in for nearly all its life. Most visitors gasp when they enter it and look around in amazement. Six windows give ample light and a great feeling of space.

Ascending the stone stairs once more, one passes a small room which has a large water tank. This was probably once a Solar. So many died in it during the taking of the castle in 1595, nobody would sleep in it thereafter. It was used for the sentries on the battlements. They had quick access to the Court Room via a small balcony.

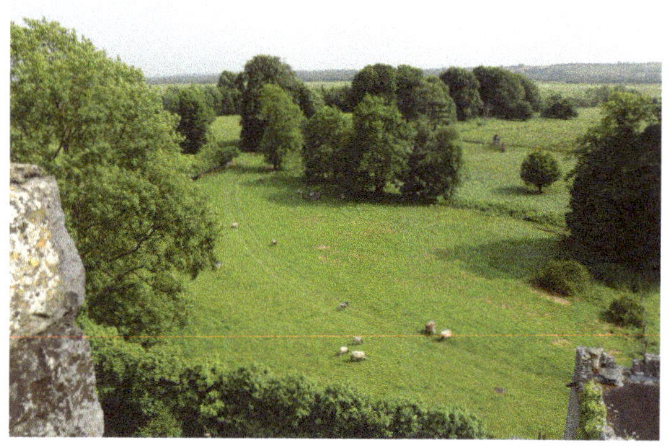
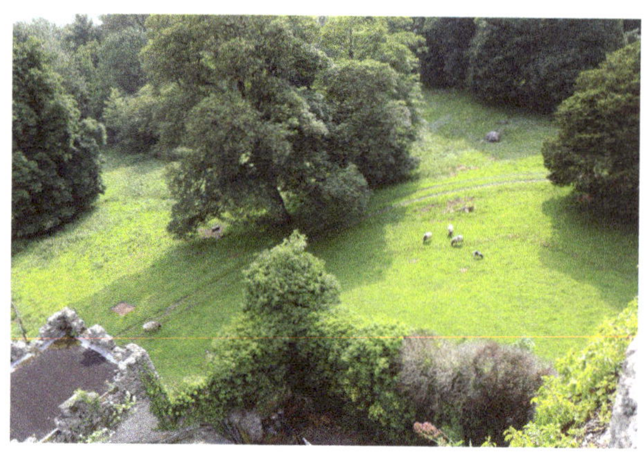
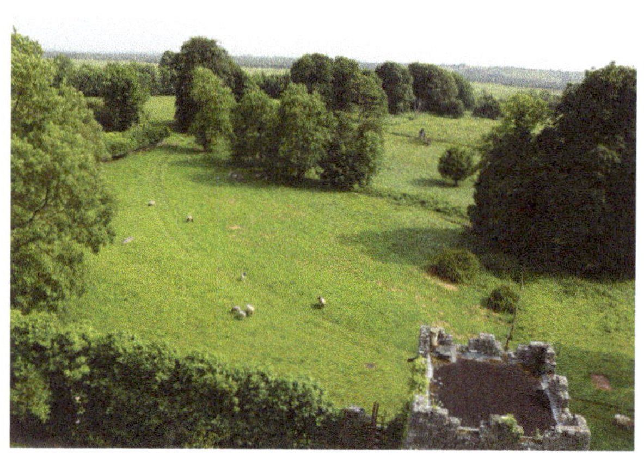
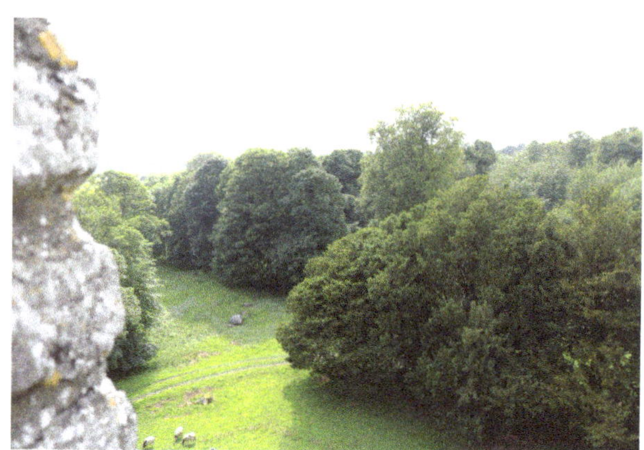
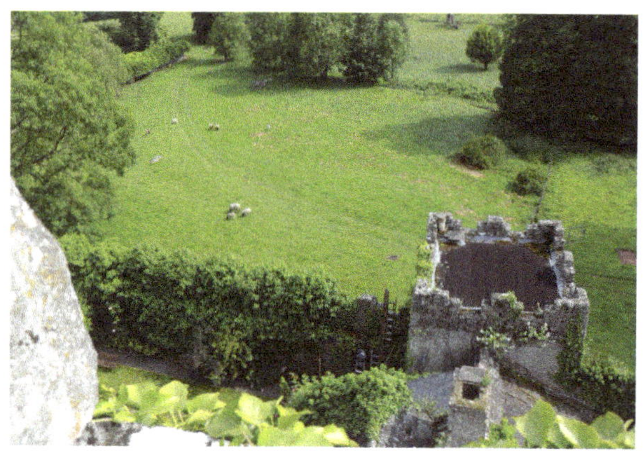
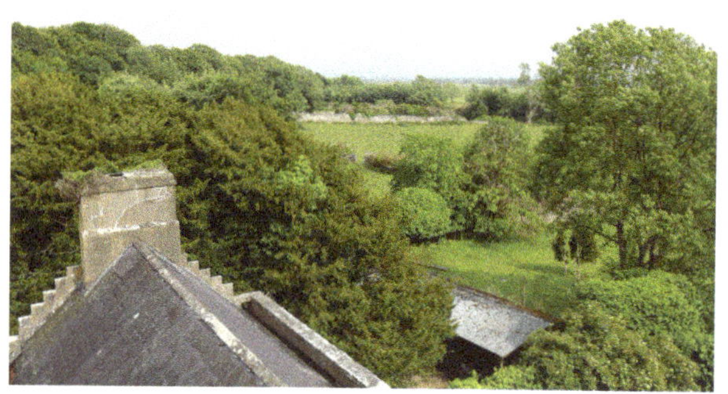

Panoramic views around the castle

Up on the battlements, 90 feet tall, the true size and nature of the building become very apparent. From such a height, one looks down on the curtain bawn wall and walled gardens and beyond them to the seventy acres of parkland. In winter, the Shannon and Little Brosna Rivers flood and create a winter lake which stretches from 50 yards from the castle to seven miles of water.

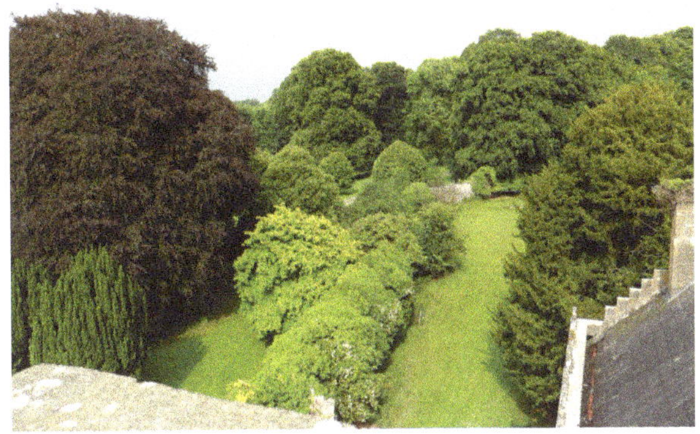

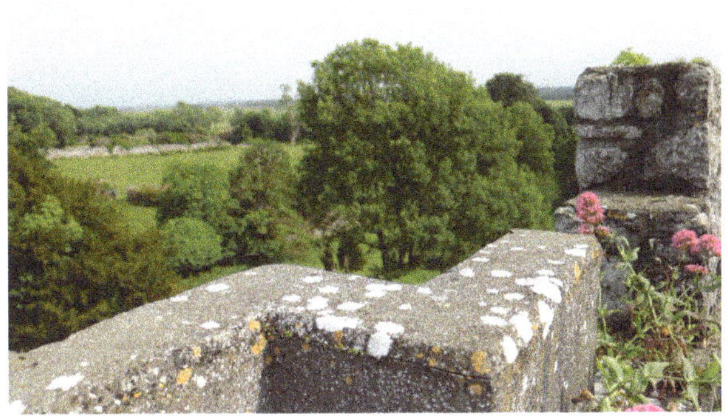

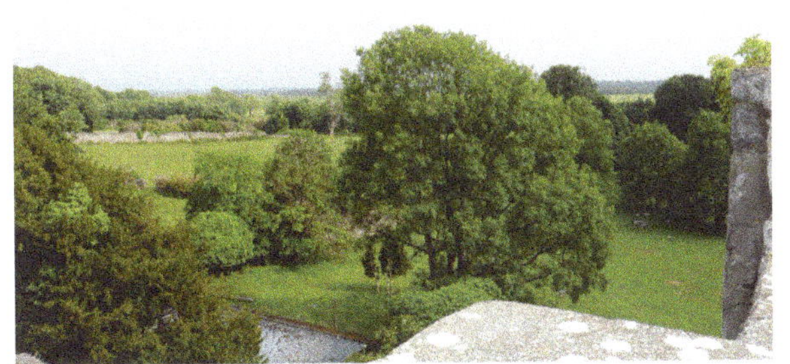

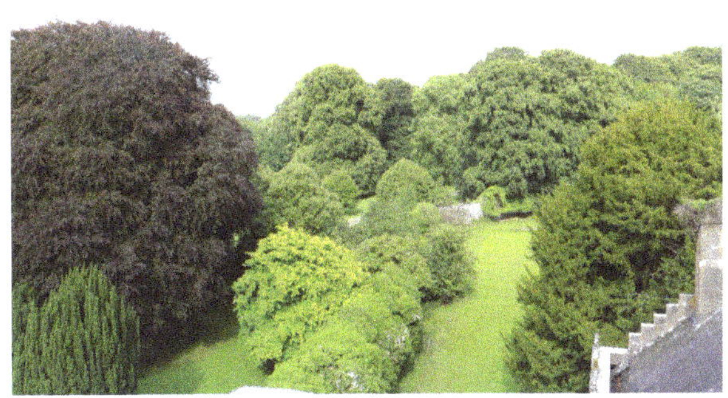

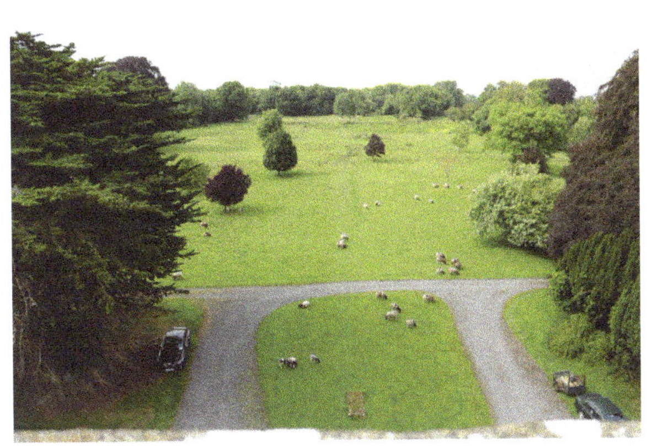

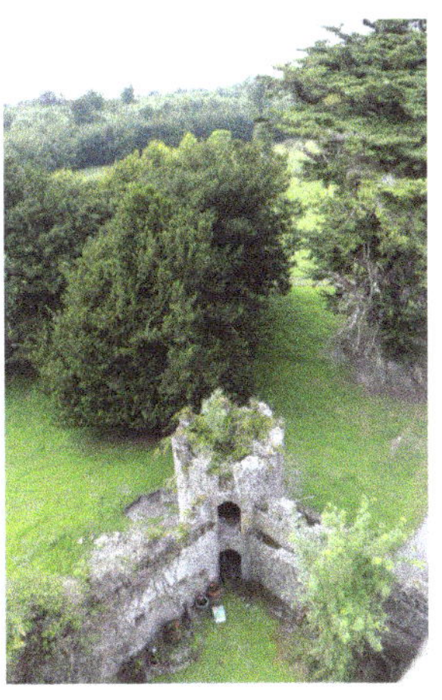

We donated our shooting rights of 1,000 acres to the government. This area is now a National Government bird sanctuary containing up to 42,000 birds. The whole valley has been designated a Natural Heritage area. Standing on the battlements, one begins to realise the impact of a medieval stone castle set in a seventy-acre park, surrounded by about 80,000 trees in a bird sanctuary in a natural heritage area. It is spectacular.

Descending the stairs, one eventually reaches a small door set in a wall and one steps through to the garderobe passageway built inside the 12-foot thick castle walls. The little room at the end was the medieval garderobe or lavatory which once had a cold stone seat.

Another door leads to a small hallway, modern bathroom and a guest bedroom. This delightful room is above the kitchen and has windows looking down on two walled gardens and the park. The roof beams here are only about 200 years old, but part of the walls have to be about 600 years older than that.

One now descends the stairs very carefully as the stair treads are of different heights. This was done when the castle was built so that attackers would stumble on them, and thus at a critical moment lose their lives with the help of a well-aimed pike.

Stepping on to the ground floor, the murder hole is above your head and facing you is the little room which has been used over many centuries as the chapel and sentry post. It is of different construction to the rest of the building and has a domed ceiling.

Next comes the Main Guard, which is now the dining room.

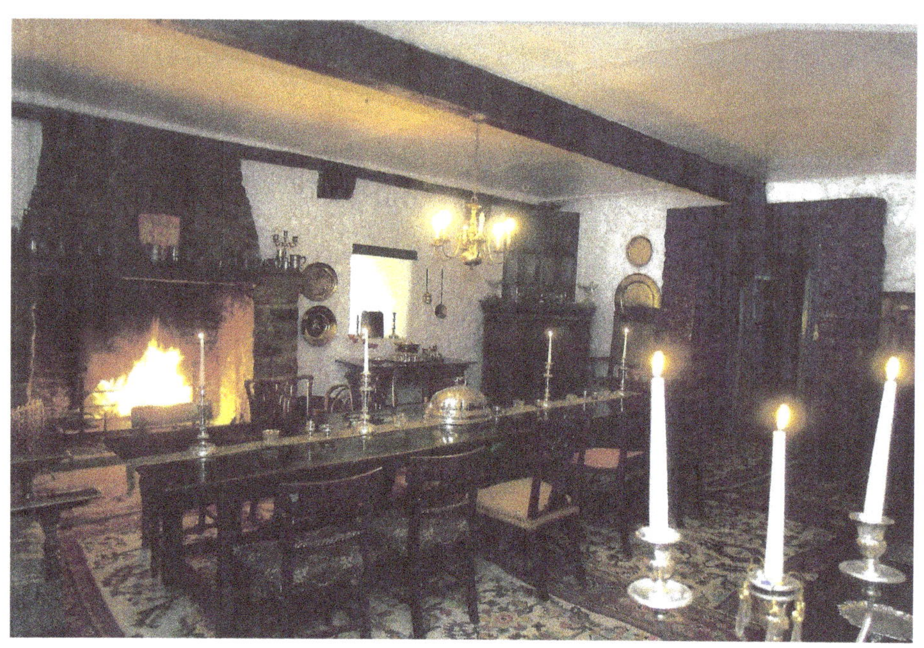

Dining room (with previous dining table, now sold!)

Ancient weapons hang on the walls, oil painted portraits over 350 years old look down on an oak table 16 feet long with a polish engendered by 300 years of beeswax. Silver candlesticks gleam from the light of a huge fire and the atmosphere of antiquity is so strong that once can almost feel the people who lived and died on this very spot for 1,400 years.

A 12 feet long brick-lined passageway leads to a room with its 300 years old flagstones under a modernised kitchen of great charm and character.

From there one passes the oil-fired boiler to a bathroom, kitchen/washroom and then into the back tower which is now an office with a storeroom above it.

In all, there are six bedrooms, one WC and basin, four full bathrooms, one Drawing Room, one Library area, one Great Hall, one Court Room, one water tank room, one Main Guard Dining Room, one Office one storeroom, two kitchens, one stone spiral stairway, one wooden stairway, two porches and corridors.

The secret of a good restoration is that when all is complete, it should look as if nothing has really changed – but it has. 3,000 feet of plumbing may not show, but they make a lot of difference to living in this day and age.

For example, the Main Guard may not look as if it has been overhauled, but it took one man one whole year to get it the way it looks today. In 1972, it was a boiler room and looked it.

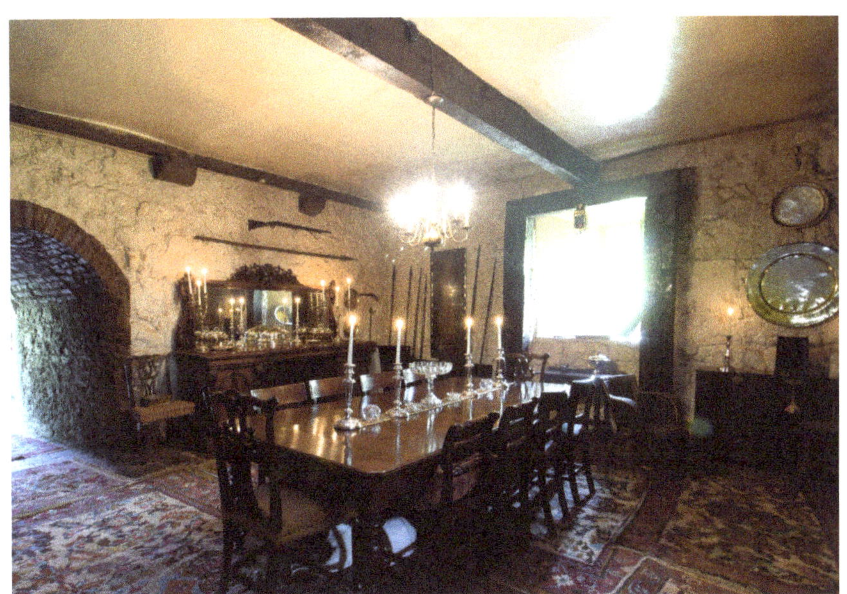

The Main Guard from another angle, without special table, but with Bob the dog ©Tina Claffey

The castle now has only 157 acres around it, but in the days of the Moore family, it had 6,000 acres. Further back in time when the O'Madden Clan Chief lived here, his kingdom stretched from here almost to Loughrea, County Galway. Even today, it takes 45 minutes by car to reach the western boundary of his kingdom.

The men and women who lived in Cloghan Castle in the past did not live poorly and they surrounded themselves with beautiful things. They dressed well and they travelled to other countries. The castle may have many fine things in it today, but it nearly always did have, making it a delightful place to live in then and now.

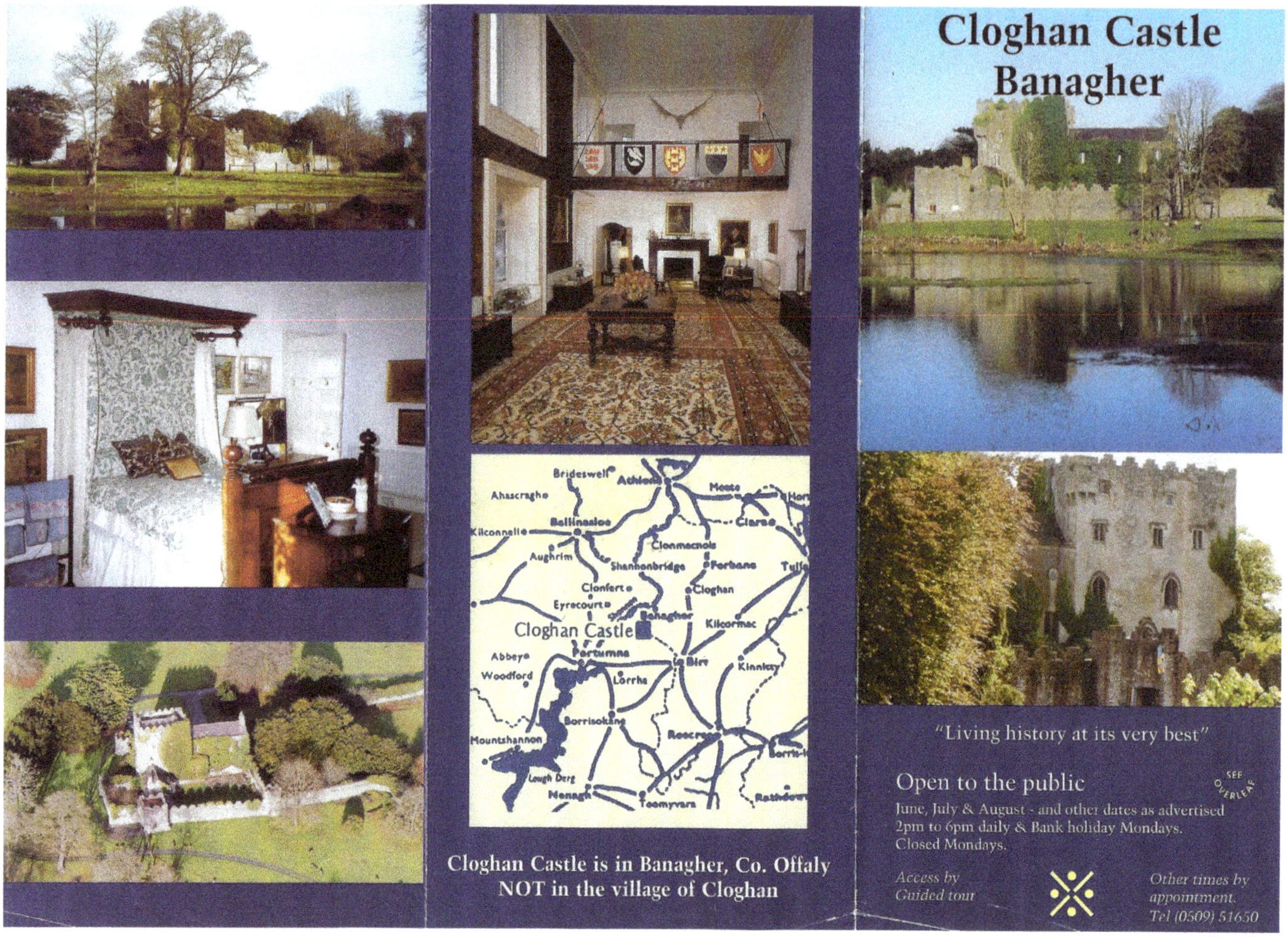

Cloghan Castle
Banagher

Cloghan Castle is in Banagher, Co. Offaly
NOT in the village of Cloghan

"Living history at its very best"

Open to the public

SEE OVERLEAF

June, July & August - and other dates as advertised
2pm to 6pm daily & Bank holiday Mondays.
Closed Mondays.

Access by
Guided tour

Other times by
appointment.
Tel (0509) 51650

Tourism Leaflet about Cloghan Castle

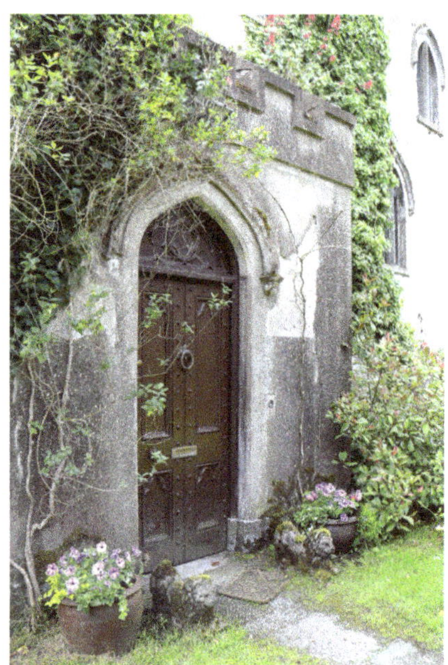

Front Door

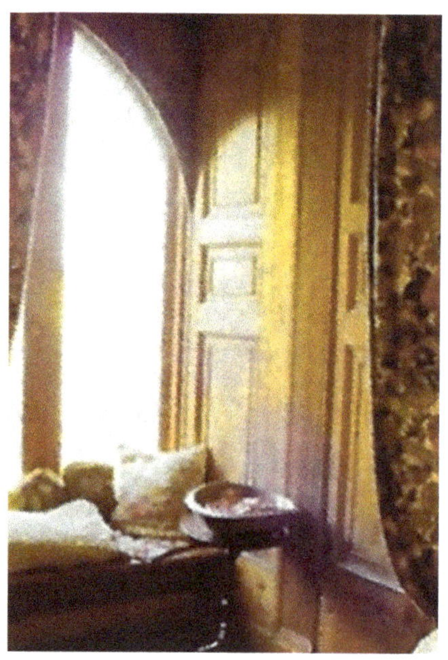

Drawing Room Window Seat

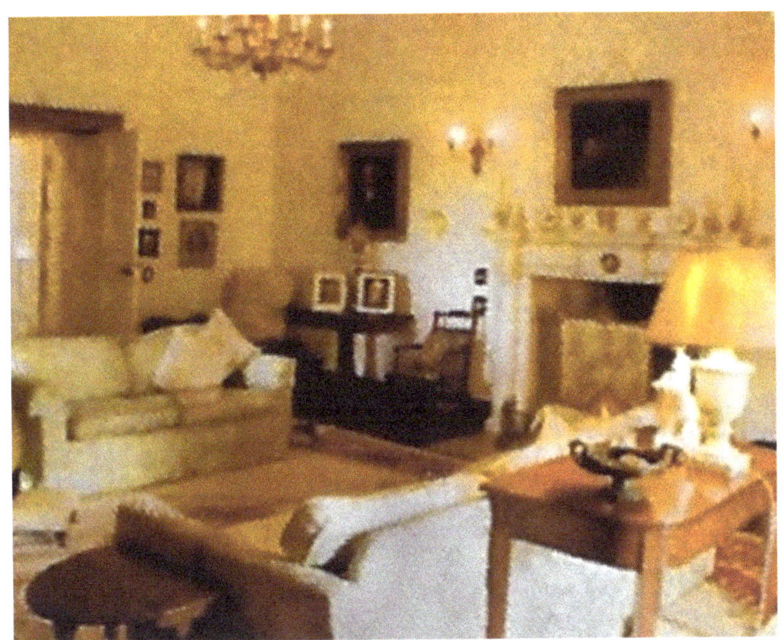

Drawing Room

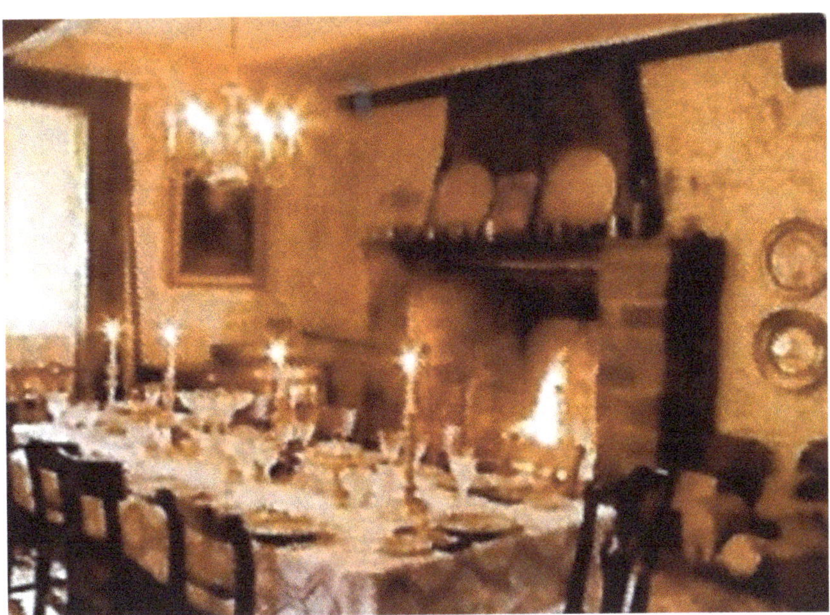

Dining Room with Candles Lit

Chapter 19

Epilogue

Epilogue

The Celtic Tiger Dies – And Takes The Country With It

The finishing of this book has taken many years mostly due to extra information arriving in bits and pieces. In 2008, the Celtic Tiger collapsed due to political corruption, uncontrolled bank lending and ensuing property development.

The Cloghan Castle estate dropped in value drastically and became impossible to sell or even rent. By 2018, the health of my wife and myself had deteriorated and our investments for old age were lost. The time had come to hand the ancient castle to someone else who would love it as we had done.

Cloghan Castle

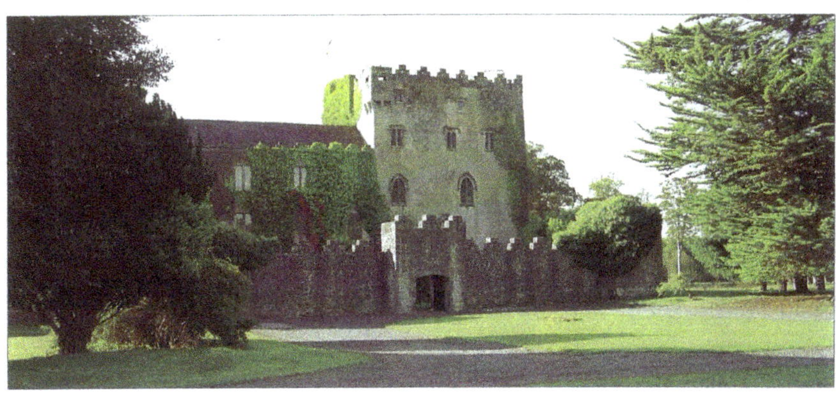

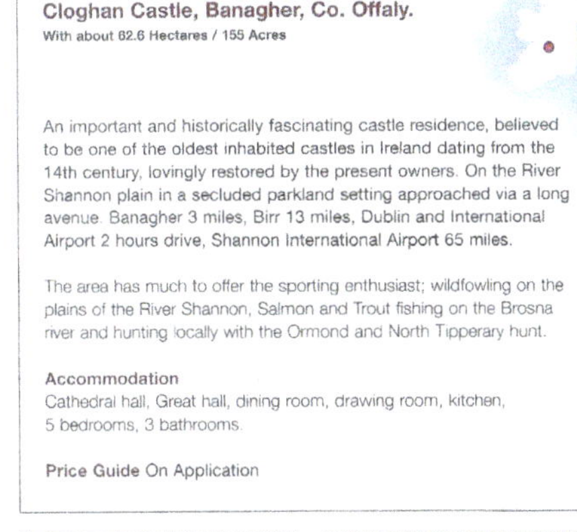

Cloghan Castle, Banagher, Co. Offaly.
With about 62.6 Hectares / 155 Acres

An important and historically fascinating castle residence, believed to be one of the oldest inhabited castles in Ireland dating from the 14th century, lovingly restored by the present owners. On the River Shannon plain in a secluded parkland setting approached via a long avenue. Banagher 3 miles, Birr 13 miles, Dublin and International Airport 2 hours drive, Shannon International Airport 65 miles.

The area has much to offer the sporting enthusiast; wildfowling on the plains of the River Shannon, Salmon and Trout fishing on the Brosna river and hunting locally with the Ormond and North Tipperary hunt.

Accommodation
Cathedral hall, Great hall, dining room, drawing room, kitchen, 5 bedrooms, 3 bathrooms.

Price Guide On Application

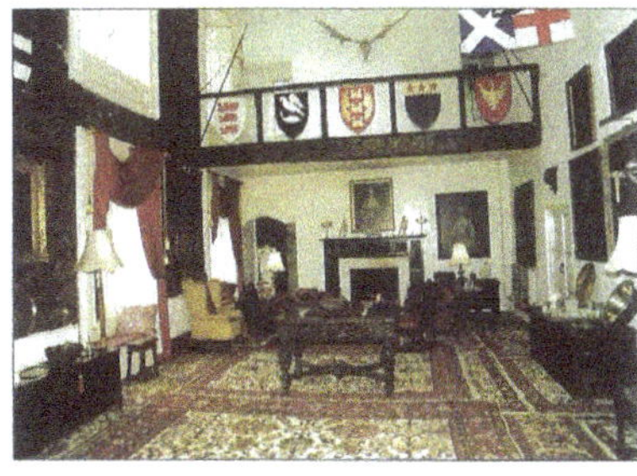

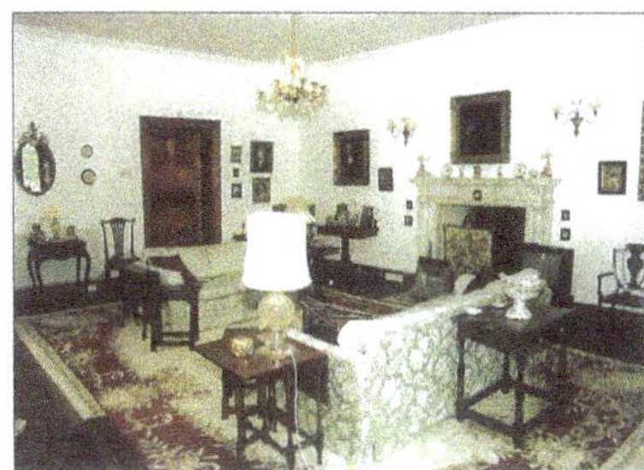

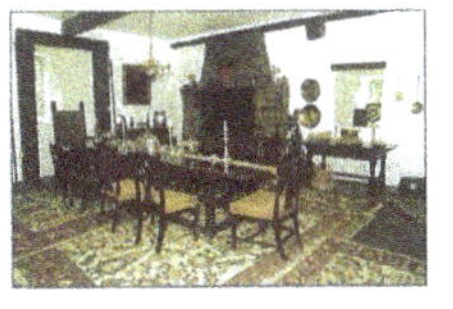

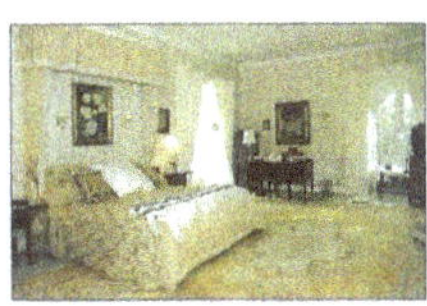

Cloghan Castle Sale Brochure

From the Editor

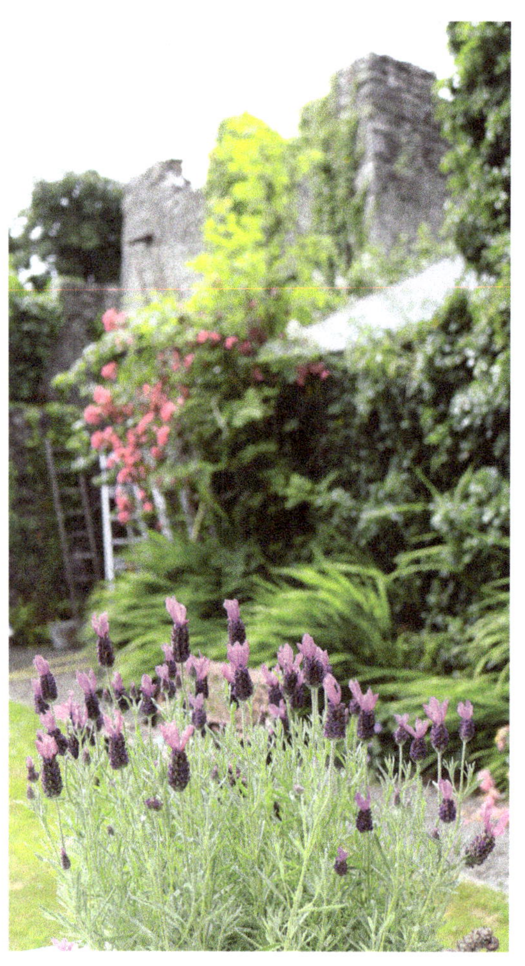

One of the Walled Gardens

Many would agree that when one thinks of Brian, one pictures him with a thoughtful, amused twinkle in his eye. His family will remember the countless times we'd see him looking down at us from sitting on top of one particular tower, waving happily while he got on with facing his personal nemesis, a stubborn roof. Our stepfather/father's chance for quiet reflection was either on his ride on mower or up there with his ever burning Bitumen hoping to finally prevent that one mysterious leak.

Elyse took refuge from the physical strains of living in a rambling monument by turning to her university studies, when she wasn't feeding a number of neighbouring youths during their hard-won tea break. For nearly 40 years, Cloghan Castle and its small estate provided two or three plucky teenagers with his/her First Summer or Saturday job, either working outside on the Desmesne, inside with Housekeeping or as Tour Guides. In the 1990s, Cloghan saw 7,000 visitors come through 45 + minute tours over the space of five afternoons a week in the summer months. Brian and Elyse enjoyed seeing those teens flourish and move on to higher education.

There were glittering parties and dinners, a Bal Masque or two, and once a 30 foot tall Christmas tree. Although the day to day atmosphere consisted of a fairly ordinary family life including ever present home cooking, much talk and often heated debate, there was also their on-call working life. This working day necessitated local ladies on staff (some of whom became good friends), farmer neighbours helping out in emergencies, and frequent unexpected visitors from far flung places. The task of keeping the Desmesne, 200 Jacob sheep, and wildlife sanctuary running well meant Cloghan was a place bursting with life.

Later, grandchildren would ride plastic tractors round the Great Hall, riding especially fast under the murder hole, then past the Chapel and into the walled garden if it was a soft rain, or, more likely than not, detour through the back kitchen. Sometimes, our parents were able to offer the space, peaceful grounds and a spare bedroom to a few people over the years needing respite.

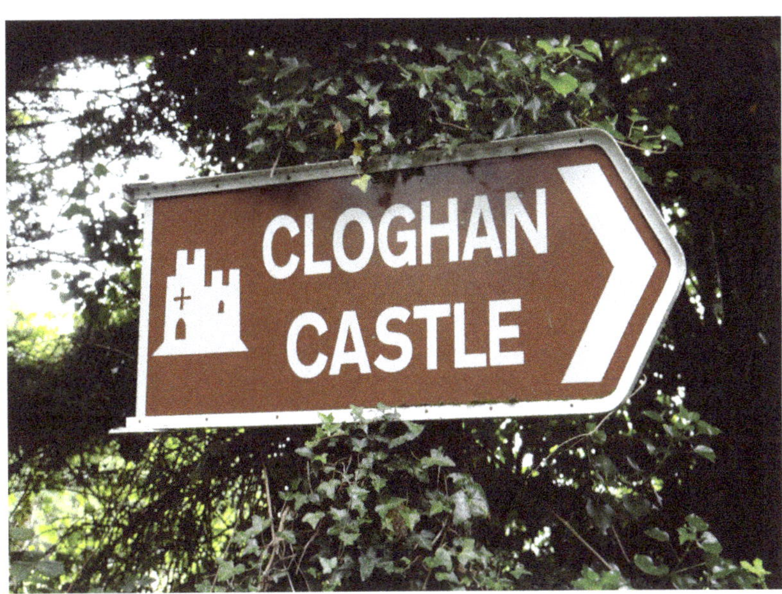

Tourism Signpost for Cloghan Castle

We are grateful our parents are now living more comfortably in a contemporary home with its necessary stair lift. We are also appreciative of those memories made together – in such an extraordinary place. May the new owners of Cloghan Castle be as richly blessed as were our parents.

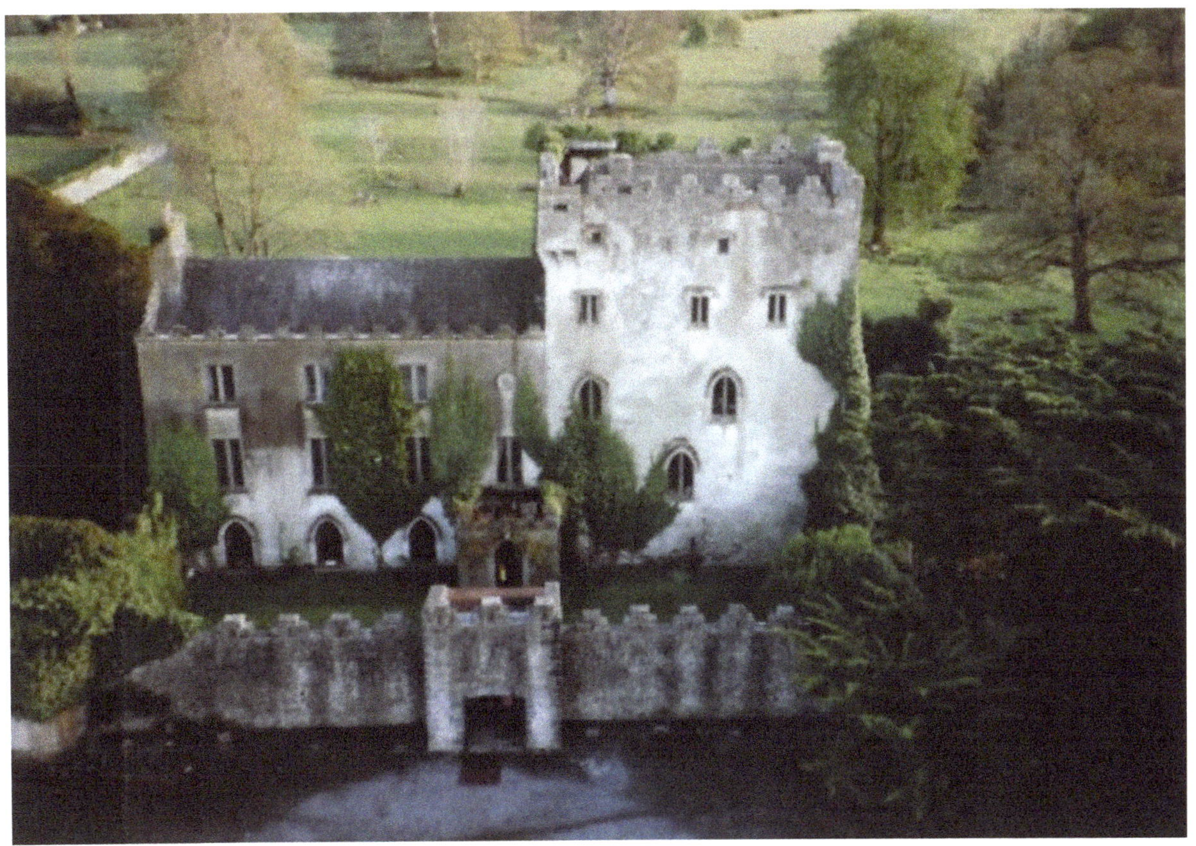

Aerial View of Cloghan Castle

Bibliography

Anderson, Jorgen, The Witch on the Wall, Medieval Erotic Sculpture in the British Isles, Rosenkilde and Bagger, Copenhagen, 1977.

Boswell, James, *The Life of Samuel Johnson*, 1791,(Extract from '*Oliver Goldsmith*'), edited by Croker, J W, 1831.

Brewer, James Norris, *Beauties of Ireland: being original delineations, topographical, historical, and biographical, of each county*, London, Sherwood, Jones, & co, 1825-1826.

Clayton, F. H., *Scenes and Incidents in Irish Life*, Montreal, John Lovell & Son, 1884.

Cooke, Jim. "The Graves Family in Ireland." Dublin Historical Record, vol. 50, no. 1, 1997, pp. 25–39. JSTOR, www.jstor.org/stable/30101157. Accessed 22 Jan. 2020.

Cooke, Thomas Lalor, *The Early History of the Town of Birr, or Parsonstown*, Robertson & Co, Dublin, 1875.

Creagh, Sir O'Moore, *The Autobiography of General Sir O'Moore Creagh, VC, GCB, GCSI*, Hutchinson, London, 1924.

Creagh VC, GCB, GCSI, The late General Sir O'Moore and Humphris, E. M., *The V.C. and D.S.O. Volume 2, The Distinguished Service Order 1886-1915*, London, The Standard Art Book Co, 1924.

Cunningham, George, *Anglo-Norman Advance into the South West Midlands of Ireland 1185-1221*, Roscrea, Parkmore Press, 1987.

De Vere White, Terence, *The Anglo-Irish*, Gollancz, 1972.

Gleeson, Reverend John, *History of Ely O'Carroll*, Robert's Books, Two Volumes, Kilkenny, 1982, 1910.

Graves, Charles, *The Bad Old Days*, Faber & Faber, London, 1951.

Hayes-McCoy, Professor Gerard, *Scots Mercenary Forces in Ireland 1564-1603*, Dublin, Burns, Oates & Washbourne Ltd, 1937.

Hogan, E H, (Editor) *The History of The Warr of Ireland From 1641 To 1653 by A British Officer of the Regiment of Sir John Clottworthy*, McGlashan & Gill, Dublin, 1873.

Madden, Dr More, *The Tribes and Customs of Hy-Many*, Irish Archaeological Society, Dublin, 1843.

Madden, Richard Robert and Thomas More, *The Memoirs Chiefly Autobiographical from 1798 to 1886*, Catholic Publishing Society Company, 1892.

Morrow, Ann, *Picnic in a Foreign Land*, Grafton Books, Glasgow, 1989.

Nolan, William and O'Neil, T P, *Offaly History and Society*, Dublin, Geography Publications, 1998.

O'Donnell, Patrick, *The Irish Faction Fighters of the 19th Century*, Anvil Books, 1975.

O'Donovan, Dr John, *The Tribes and Customs of Hy Many*, Dublin, Irish Archaeological Society, 1843.

Robertson, Nora, *Crowned Harp, Memories of the Last Years of the Crown in Ireland,* Dublin, Figgis, 1960.

Wilkins, Philip A., *The History of the Victory Cross, London*, Archibald Constable & Co, 1904.

Other Resources:

Papers from the Royal Society of Antiquaries of Ireland

Journals of Galway Historical Society

Journals of Mayo Historical Society

Burkes' Landed Gentry of Ireland

The Lynch-Blosse Papers

The O'Madden Family Tree

The Clanricarde Family Tree

RTE Guide, March 14th 1986

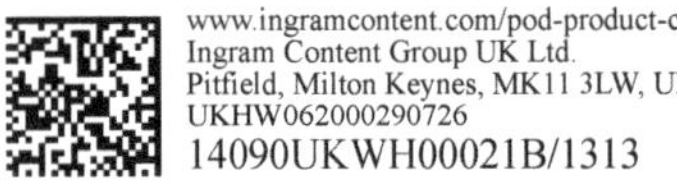
www.ingramcontent.com/pod-product-compliance
Ingram Content Group UK Ltd.
Pitfield, Milton Keynes, MK11 3LW, UK
UKHW062000290726
14090UKWH00021B/1313

9 781912 328598